COUNSELING GEMS

Thoughts for the Practitioner

James P. Carnevale, Ph.D.
Professor of Counseling
San Diego State University

ACCELERATED DEVELOPMENT INC.
Publishers
Muncie Indiana

COUNSELING GEMS: THOUGHTS FOR THE PRACTITIONER

2 3 4 5 6 7 8 9 10

Printed in the United States of America

Technical Development: Tanya Dalton
Delores Kellogg
Marguerite Mader
Sheila Sheward

Library of Congress Cataloging-in-Publication Data

Carnevale, James P., 1931-
Counseling gems : thoughts for the practitioner / James P. Carnevale.
p. cm.
ISBN 0-915202-88-3
1. Counseling. I. Title
BF637.C6C346 1989
158'.3--dc20 89-6588
CIP

LCN: 89-6588

ACCELERATED DEVELOPMENT INC.
PUBLISHERS
3808 West Kilgore Avenue
Muncie, Indiana 47304-4896
Toll Free Order Number 1-800-222-1166

INTRODUCTION

This manual happened because my practicum students wanted it to happen. My usual way of teaching practicum was to respond to the counseling process in which the students were involved. My responses were usually of two kinds: (1) how to think about the situations and (2) what to do about the situations. The latter type of response was so client-counselor specific that it seemed to have no obvious generalizability. But the first type of response, how to think about the situations, did seem generalizable and students began writing down these kinds of responses and sharing them with each other. We began to jokingly call them "Carnevale's Pearls of Wisdom." At the end of the semester's practicum the students would often create a humorous card, filled with these "pearls" and accompanied by funny drawings that captured the ideas but with an interesting and humorous twist. This became almost a tradition for my practicum and I started to save them for "memory days."

As these cards accumulated, I began to see my "pearls in a new way—in a more organized way. I wondered what their notes looked like and I asked to see them. They were glad to share them with me. They suggested that I put them all together in some kind of a binder and have students purchase them. I did go so far as to put them in some kind of order; but I was reluctant to do any more. Several students asked to see what I had done with their notes; they liked them; and they insisted that I get them printed. So I did. My colleagues then suggested that they had an appeal beyond my practicum and urged me to get them published. So I did. This manual is the result.

James P. Carnevale

James P. Carnevale

CONTENTS

SECTION I

COUNSELING PHILOSOPHY

Points of View

1

Counseling is helping people become aware of how they are creating their lives, based upon a belief system they have forgotten they believe.

The important parts of this forgotten belief system are (1) the way they define themselves, (2) the way they define the world (people), and (3) conclusions about how best to deal with these two realities (which they have created). All present relationships are based upon these old definitions, which I believe are made very early in life. All present relationships are made to fit these early definitions and conclusions, much like the Procrustean bid of early mythology. For this reason I often say that people are living their lives based upon their own mythologies. They try to make their daily lives fit these myths, which they have created. They run into difficulty when the myths no longer seem to fit, and they must distort reality to fit their myths to such a degree that their lives become non-functional or have too much pain. Counseling is a vehicle for bringing these myths back to awareness or consciousness, to examine them, to reaffirm them or modify them to fit the reality of today rather than the reality of yesterday.

Myths are a necessary part of the human condition. They are not a bad thing, as such. But they must be based upon a current reality, not an ancient one. I tell my students that functional myths-to-live-by must develop in harmony with reality, not in dissonance with it.

2

You must have filters through which to sift and organize all the "stuff" the client gives to you.

Most beginning counselors live in fear that their first client won't talk very much and they won't have anything to work with. This happens once in a while, but not very often. A much more common problem is having a client who *does* talk and gives you so much data you drown in it. A person cannot *not* communicate. The client is always sending off information. The counselor's biggest problem is figuring out what to do with all of it. I always tell my students this, but they never believe me—until after they see a few clients.

With most clients there is so much stuff to deal with, the first problem is deciding what to ignore and throw away. The second problem is organizing the stuff you're going to keep. The third problem is then deciding what to do with what you *have* organized. The fourth problem is actually doing what you hope to do. The rest is easy.

Problems 1 and 2 can be solved only if you have a theory of personality and theory of counseling through which you see and hear your client. I think of these theories as filter systems which help me sift the wheat from the chaff. There is *so* much information coming at me, I can't possibly attend to all of it. So I put my filters in front of my eyes and my ears and largely ignore whatever can't make it through the filters. My beliefs about people and about counseling help me to screen out the irrelevant and allow me to focus my energy on data that I believe are significant for me as a counselor. That is why theories are important to the practicing counselor as well as the academician. I teach theories of personality and theories of counseling because I believe that you need these theories to build your filters to see and hear your clients. They are far more than an academic exercise. They are the basis of counseling competence. You can't begin to solve problems 1 and 2 without them. Problems 3 and 4 I'll discuss in other sections.

3

The reason persons are not solving their life problems is not because they aren't smart enough but rather is because they are working with the wrong data.

But real clients are clients because something is wrong with how they relate to people. They are resistant; they often sabotage. Their defense mechanisms are their first line of defense. With many clients a honeymoon period exists at the start of counseling that in many ways resembles the pretend clients of fellow students. But after the honeymoon is over, the work begins. So don't the disappointed or surprised when your client stops being the easy client with whom to work. If clients' problems were easy ones, they would have solved them before they came to you. Clients *are* clients because their problems are difficult. The mistake they make in human relationships they are going to make with you. When they do, be prepared to use it therapeutically. But it won't be easy. . . .

4

The power of positive thinking only works for those people who are already happy.

Many people, including clients, think that "If I'd just try harder at being happy, I'd be happy." It doesn't work that way. Telling someone to cheer up has never helped them to feel cheery. Telling persons to stop putting themselves down has never lessened their feeling bad about themselves. In the Peanuts cartoon, Lucy's therapy is meant to be a joke. In real life, that kind of therapy is no laughing matter.

5

Real clients are seldom easy clients with whom to work. If something significant wasn't wrong with them, they wouldn't be clients at all.

In most counselor training programs, student counselors usually begin by working with fellow students, as they make their first attempts at developing counseling skills. Their fellow students usually try to be "good" clients. They are cooperative, they are pleasant, they try to give the student counselor something with which to work. The pretend client is normally straightforward. Because they rarely deal with an actual lifestyle flaw, they rarely resort to unconscious defense mechanisms to defeat the counselor's attempts to do therapy. On the contrary, they very overtly try to help them in the process. The student counselor easily can like the pretend client as skills are practiced. How nice being a counselor is.

But real clients are clients because something is wrong with how they relate to people. They are resistant; they often sabotage. Their defense mechanisms are their first line of defense. With many clients a honeymoon period exists at the start of counseling that in many ways resembles the pretend clients of fellow students. But after the honeymoon is over, the work begins. So don't the disappointed or surprised when your client stops being the easy client with whom to work. If clients' problems were easy ones, they would have solved them before they came to you. Clients *are* clients because their problems are difficult. The mistake they make in human relationships they are going to make with you. When they do, be prepared to use it therapeutically. But it won't be easy. . . .

6

Clients are better at being clients than most counselors are at being counselors.

Clients have been practicing being who and what they are for years—as many years as they are old. Therefore they are experts at it. They also are experts at defending themselves from the counselor's attempts to introduce the element of change—the important ingredient of therapy. So be prepared for the client's success at undermining and sabotaging your therapeutic interventions. Freud called this resistance, about 100 years ago, and most counselors still don't understand the process.

7

A 5 degree or 10 degree shift in the situation can be significant. A shift of 180 degrees is probably phony and won't last.

Because I believe therapeutic change is ultimately a change in the client's style of living, I believe that change in lifestyle will not be a large one. But that is all right; a 5 degree or 10 degree change will be enough. A person who has been a "doormat" for the world will probably not become a charismatic leader because of therapy. But the client may become a nice person who knows how to say "no." An aggressive, abrasive person will probably not become everybody's friend. But the client may well become an intense, confident individual who is OK to be around. The client who has always found the other person's weak spot and then exploited it to his or her own advantage won't become a do-gooder. But the client may well feel less threatened in his or her own right and be able to use a power of analysis to be a good problem solver to have around.

Most clients, after they have identified their lifestyle and found how they contribute to their problems because of it, usually hope to change it 180 degrees. The "quiet one" hopes to become the life of the party; the overbearing one hopes to be the great mediator; the seductress hopes to be the great mind. The counselor must help the client to see that changes of this magnitude are not real and won't last. We can't change our stripes completely. But we don't have to. A 5 degree or 10 degree change can be enough.

8

All behavior has meaning and purpose in *some* context. Nothing is an accident.

Behavior is *always* directed at accomplishing something. Freud said it 100 years ago, and it is as important a truth today as it was then. One of the important pieces of data to help your client discover is his or her unconscious intentions in daily life. How can you make sense out of apparently crazy behavior?

Example: I once had a client who was a real estate broker. The time was the middle 1970s here in Southern California. Real estate was increasing in value at an incredible rate. Everyone who was able to do so was investing in real estate and making very good profits. Everyone except my client. He was making money for all of his clients; but for himself, he was doing very badly. It didn't make sense. He knew his business, and yet with his own money he seemed to be making stupid mistakes, making little profit—in some cases even losing money. I assumed he was doing poorly for a good reason. *He was doing too good a job at doing poorly* for what was happening to be an accident. Further exploration revealed that although he said he loved his wife very much and was a very lucky man to have such a wife, in fact he resented her very much. He thought she dominated his life and was "always right." He never could win an argument with her; and yet she was so good to him, he felt guilty about feeling resentful about her. But she had one flaw in her armor—she loved money. She loved his financial success and really enjoyed spending his "hard earned income." What better way to defeat his wife than to lose money so she couldn't enjoy her great pleasure? That is exactly what he was doing. As soon as I began seeing them in marriage counseling and he began to find more appropriate ways of dealing with his marriage problems, he stopped making his "crazy" mistakes, and his earnings increased accordingly. His mistakes weren't mistakes. The were perfect behaviors for his secret intention.

9

Habits become habits because they accomplish something very well.

Whenever I draw clients' attention to particular speech patterns that they use often or to physical patterns of behavior such as the positioning of hands or the way they roll their eyes on numerous occasions, more often than not they are apt to say, "It is just a habit; I've done it for years"—and then wants to drop the subject and get on to more important things. I never just drop the subject because the client has labeled something a habit. I agree with him or her. Of course it is a habit! But habits become habits because the accomplish something very well. I want to find out what this particular habit is accomplishing. Inevitable we can determine what a habit does for the client, and it is often an important part of the person's lifestyle.

Now, I realize that many mannerisms run in families or even cultures. At first glance, one might assume that one picks up the habit simply by association—as one does a speech accent or a way of walking. But I assume that an individual picks up not only the mannerism but the *use* of the mannerism or habit that the family or culture has developed—usually at an unconscious level of understanding. Determining the use of a habit is many times an important piece of information in the process of counseling. Don't drop the subject simply because it is a habit.

10

Defense mechanisms are chosen and maintained because they work so well.

Freud postulated that people unconsciously develop defense mechanisms in order to create a reality which they can handle. They deny or distort reality so that it fits the myths by which they believe they must live. I am firmly convinced that Freud was right. I believe that one of the important tasks of counseling or therapy is to uncover these defense mechanisms and help the client to deal with reality in a more realistic and functional way. But the clients *are* well defended. They really believe in their denials and distortions and they have developed their unique way of denying or distorting reality in ways that make sense and that really work for them. Because their denials and distortions work so well is why friends and loved ones have not been able to help clients help themselves. Defense mechanisms work because they help the client avoid pain, fear, or anger. The avoidance is the reinforcement that maintains the behavior. Breaking through these defense behaviors is a formidable task indeed—but an absolutely crucial task, if counseling is to succeed.

11

No all/nothings exist except for being pregnant.

Most clients seems to be living their lives as though some aspect of their life is an all or nothing situation.

"If I'm not agreeable, people won't like me."

"If I'm nice to people they'll take advantage of me."

"I think people ask to be misled."

"Women are. . . ."

"Men are. . . ."

"Either I can trust him or I can't."

"I'm not acceptable unless I. . . ."

Whenever I come upon one of these absolute beliefs in a client I find it to be an important part of a faulty belief system, and the behavior that follows from this belief system is always an important part of the relationship system that is faulty. The absolute, all-or-nothing aspect of the belief has usually been forgotten by the client, and the effect of the faulty belief is seldom seen as contributing to the relationship difficulty. But challenging the all/nothing thought and modifying it to fit reality gives the client some wiggle room to modify the behavior and the relationships.

Usually several of these all or nothing spots exist in clients. They are always "sick" spots. Don't let them go unchallenged and always tie them somehow to a faulty relationship. It can be the start of improvement in their life.

12

Remember that in counseling the problem is always sitting in the chair across from you. . . and so is the solution!!!

I make a very strong distinction between the process of counseling and that of social work. Both are important. We need the social worker to help a client learn to better work "the system," to redress inequalities and the problems that are indeed the result of an unfair and often unjust environment. Victims of the unscrupulous need aid in stopping unscrupulous behavior being used against them. Finding the means of getting food, shelter, or protection are all areas in which an individual needs the kind of service that the social workers can do so well.

But clients of counseling need help of an entirely different sort. They need help in discovering how *they* are creating *their* part in what is wrong in their life. Clients of counseling need help in discovering their unconscious goals and intentions, which I believe is their therapeutic problem. That is why we have developed the old cliche: "Only you can solve or resolve your problem." I do not see the role of counseling as helping the client to find a job or learn to keep a budget. The role of counseling is to help the client to discover how they prevented themselves from learning these skills in the first place.

13

**Counseling is the TRUTH BUSINESS. . .
and the truth is hard to find.**

Counseling is usually the last place people come for help with the pain in their life. Before they see a counselor, they have talked over their problem with their friends, with their spouse, with their priest or minister. And they should have! For one thing, these people don't charge for their time—and it only makes sense to try free, first. For some of the problems people have, these friends or ministers can indeed be of real help. By all means, these sources of help *should* be utilized first. A client would be crazy not to try these sources first, and I don't work with crazy people. So when I see someone as a client for the first time, I assume they have already tried various people before me. And I also assume that if these other folks haven't been helpful, the reason isn't because they aren't good problem solvers. I assume they have been working on the wrong problems, or try to solve the problem with the wrong data, or both. What I do that friends and relatives don't do is that I look for the unconscious aspects of the client's life. I look for defense mechanisms, denials, distortions, projections, and repressions. I look for hidden truths that are playing such an important part in the client's life. I realize that these truths *are* hidden, the client has been unable to solve or resolve problems that are causing the pain. When we find the true variables of an issue, or when we find the true issue itself, the client can then usually solve or resolve what must be solved or resolved and live his or her life in a more satisfying manner. But these truths are not self-evident. These truths are hard to find.

14

Clients are seldom helpless.
They have developed strange ways of succeeding.

One of my difficult tasks as a practicum supervisor is teaching student-counselors to avoid the trap of feeling sorry for their clients or wanting to rescue them from the plight in which they present themselves. The counselor will have difficulty in not feeling sorry for clients who seems to be helpless in their misery or their pain—and the misery or the pain is very real. The key point is that *they are not helpless.* On the contrary, they are probably being successful! Successful because, at any given moment in time, people are choosing how they are responding to the world. These choices are largely unconscious ones based upon unconscious assumptions, but they are choices, nevertheless. Being helpless victims of certain circumstances is a choice that clients have been making for some time. Clients do not experience that they are choosing to be helpless; and as we begin counseling I don't know the reasons they are choosing to be helpless. But I assume that during the counseling process clients and I will come to understand that they *are* so choosing and the reasons behind this choice. Rather than feeling sorry for clients, I want my students to feel curious: curious about how clients have managed to avoid finding the solution to their problems, curious about clients' self-concept and concept of the circumstances in which they are living; curious about finding new options by which clients will live their lives.

This curiosity must be experienced by the client as a part of a warm and caring human being. I am not advocating that student counselors view their clients with the detached curiosity of a laboratory scientist. But I am advocating that they view clients as people who need help in understanding the pieces of the puzzle of their life, not as someone who needs their sympathy.

15

When a client agrees with you, that doesn't mean you are right; when they disagree with you, that doesn't mean you're wrong.

Because I believe that so much of the initial counseling process is uncovering the client's unconscious processes and motivation, I don't believe the client's conscious agreement or disagreement is the best validation for my early assumptions or hunches. Then, too, some clients have a style of agreeing with figures of authority, regardless of their own opinions. Others seem determined to disagree, no matter what. In any case, the client's agreement or disagreement with the counselor, while not to be ignored, does not have the significance for me that it might have for many.

However, a crucial issue is for the counselor not argue with the client—the client can to easily win an argument by not coming back. Also, if you do argue you run the danger of contributing to the delinquency of your client, which I discuss in another section of this book.

16

People are not weak—they're just not in touch with their power.

The perfect excuse for why clients can't change themselves or parts of their lives is that they aren't strong enough. Mind you, they would if they could, but they are just too weak. If only they were stronger, or had more will power, or were more self-disciplined, or had more determination . . . but since they weren't born with enough of these good things, what seems to remain is that they are destines to remain the same. What a shame.

Nuts! I don't believe any of it! A person chooses. And they choose in light of what they want or intend. They are always doing what they want to do (except perhaps in the case of addiction—but that is another story) and being weak and having no will power has nothing to do with it; they are simple excuses to attempt avoiding being held accountable for the choices they are making—and which they are making with great power, strength, and determination!

17

However you are feeling about the client or are responding to the client is probably what the client intended.

This truism is one of the most important, but it is also one of the most difficult to understand and accept. For years students have been taught to thing that how they perceive the world and respond to it is their problem. At least 50 percent of any personal interaction is their responsibility. They are choosing and creating their responses. And it is true. *But* the counseling relationship is a very special one and some special rules apply. Because the counselor has duties and responsibilities unlike those of other relationships, the counselor should enter the relationship as close to a "blank screen" as possible. Instead of defending or putting forth his or her position, the counselor should initially aim for remaining neutral and allowing the client to impinge upon the counselor. This is my definition of an initial professional stance. I try to be neutral in messages I know I am sending to the client; I try to reveal as little about myself as I can without being "strange" or distant. I deliberately attempt to elicit the client's style of meeting a new situation and tune my antennae to what he or she does and what the client seems to be hoping for from me. By what the client seems to be trying to elicit from me, I have important clues develop that tell me about him or her. If, for instance, I find myself sorry for the client, it is probably because the client tries to get people to feel sorry for him or her, to help the person, or to not expect too much from him, etc., etc. If I find myself feeling annoyed by the client it is probably because the client knows how to deal with people who are annoyed with her and puts them in this stance as quickly as possible. Some people can deal only with others who are in a position of either more or less power than they. This will be manifested in the counseling relationship *very* quickly and is likely to be an important variable in the therapeutic process.

What I am trying to communicate here is not that the counselor be phoney and not that the counselor be non-human. Instead, I am advocating that the counselor be very much in touch with his or her humanness, but with a different twist. Instead of merely responding to the client, as would the person on the street, I suggest the counselor be aware of how he or she *wants* to respond to the client, and then make a professional judgment call about how to use this information.

A recent example that I think illustrates a part of what I'm trying to say was a woman in her 30s who was working with a student counselor. She came into the counseling room and began to talk about how she seemed to allow people to impose their will upon her. However, she soon began changing the furniture arrangement in the room, insisted that the counselor and she should sit in different positions than the counselor had arranged, and generally took over the situation. The student counselor was flabbergasted, a bit annoyed with the client, and remained quite ineffective with the client for the rest of the interview.

To me several things became evident. The client appeared to project her bossiness onto others and quickly moved to be boss in the situation. She disarmed the student counselor with her aggressive behavior and managed to be left alone during the interview. Not surprising, later in the counseling relationship, the client acknowledged that she was quite lonely, had no real friends, but that by God no one ever treated her the way her mother had been treated. By allowing her a free rein and observing how she handled the situation, by keeping in check the counselor's natural responses to her behavior, we could see the diagram of her lifestyle the client gave us and an example of her problem.

18

A counseling relationship has several stages. The honeymoon is the fun part; then the work begins.

One of the unfortunate side effects of using audiovisual materials to show and demonstrate counseling or therapy sessions is that they give wrong impression of the long-term counseling relationship. Students benefit from watching an expert at work. The demonstration is usually a very good one (or they would have destroyed it and used another) and it is apt to be dramatic—that is the most marketable product. This can be misleading because

1. the session is out of context to the entire process,

2. the long term effect is completely guessed at,

3. one gets the impression that all good sessions are dramatic,

4. the repetitiousness of the process is not seen,

5. the small steps that accumulate toward significant but small personality change are not in evidence,

6. the client's attempts to sabotage the process is rarely a part of the demonstration, and

7. the various stages of the counseling process cannot be included.

All of this is because of the nature of the demonstration material; it cannot be helped. So the practicum experience must bring a fuller reality to the student counselor, which unfortunately usually comes near the conclusion of the formal educational program.

19

Counselors lose more clients by doing too little too late than by doing too much too soon.

Somewhere students counselors have picked up the idea that clients must be "ready" to begin counseling and that before they are ready a time period must be spent together, the counselor and the client, in order to establish THE RELATIONSHIP. And so they spend several sessions "getting to know each other," avoiding touchy issues and being friendly—waiting for the client to be "ready." My experience as a practicum supervisor is that after the client has come to two or three sessions and has done with the counselor only what she or he has done with neighbors or friends, the client stops coming. If being with the counselor seems to be no different than talking to friends, the client will go back to talking with friends. The friends are often more convenient to meet, and the friends probably serve coffee. I wish I had a dollar for each time student counselors thought that next time they would start the counseling and no next time ever came. The client stopped coming because nothing had been happening.

Apparently a belief floats around the halls that if the counselor starts right in counseling, the client will be frightened off and never come back—that the client can't handle "too much" and must be handled very gently. It's not true! Clients are rarely frightened off because counseling is to tough to handle. For one thing, student counselors aren't good enough counselors to move to truly sensitive areas in the first few sessions. They aren't skillful enough to go beyond what clients will allow. As I've said in another context, the client is better at being the client than the student is at being the counselor. My experience is that the client is often the one who is bringing the student-counselor along. If anyone is not ready to move to the counseling process immediately, probably the student counselor is the one.

SECTION II
GOALS and BOUNDARIES of COUNSELING

20

The counseling relationship has a unique set of parameters which carry a unique set of permissions.

The counseling relationship is unlike any other that I can think of. Its very uniqueness brings with it a unique set of parameters, a unique set of permissions for both the client and the counselor. The client seldom is consciously aware of these parameters as the relationship begins. The responsibility of the counselor is to teach them—usually in an inductive rather than a deductive way—usually by example rather than by a lecture. The following are examples of the unique parameters mentioned above:

1. Counseling is a strange combination of a formal, professional, "proper" relationship combined with an intimate, deeply personal relationship. The client has a right to expect professional knowledge used in a responsible way that is manifested in a caring, almost friend-to friend manner. But it is not really friendship. To me, friendship is a relationship of equals on some important bases. Counseling is not one of equals in the area that brings the partners together. The counselor must be in a position of greater power and control; the client must acknowledge this difference; and yet this different distribution of power must not be a stumbling block to the intimacy which the relationship requires.

2. In most intimate relationships there is a balance between the self disclosure of the principals involved. The material disclosed has usually both an historical and a current component. In the counseling relationship this balance does not exist. Different counselors use different amounts of their own self-disclosure, but I've

never seen it to be equal to that of the client. For myself, self-disclosure is usually limited to the here-and now of the counseling session.

3. Related to the above, but somewhat different, is focus. In most intimate relationships the focus of interest also balances itself out. There is a nearly equal distribution of center-stageness between principals. Not so with counseling. The relationship exists because the client needs help. The client, then, should be the center of focus. When it starts equaling itself out, the relationship is about to end—counseling is no longer necessary.

4. Intimate relationships usually benefit both partners equally. I do not believe this is so in counseling. Certainly the counselor benefits from the relationship in terms of money, feelings of success, his or her own sense of humanness. But the relationship exists because the client is not living well. Something is definitely wrong in his or her life, and the client comes to counseling to make it better. The client should benefit more than the counselor in this regard. If the counselor needs therapeutic help, then the counselor should seek professional help. The therapeutic benefits belong to the client.

The uniqueness of the counseling relationship also carries some very special permissions for the client and counselor:

1. The counselor may ask personal questions about intimate data very early in the relationship—very often in the first session, certainly in the second.

2. The counselor may direct the client to talk about subject matter the client would normally avoid.

3. The counselor need not carry on "his or her half" of a dialogue, as is characteristic of most conversations.

4. The counselor may choose to answer or not answer direct questions which the client may ask. The counselor has more control of this factor than is true of most relationships.

5. The counselor need not be restricted to polite behavior or good manners. He or she has the responsibility to challenge, to insist, to say unpleasant but true things, to stop "story telling," to cut through justifications and rationalizations, to deny the client unwarranted "face," to interrupt, to do whatever is necessary to deal with truth—whatever that might be.

I am not suggesting that the counselor has a license to abuse the client; but the counselor does have the freedom to do things that are not appropriate in normal social discourse.

21

All problems in counseling are relationship problems. Period!

An extremely helpful procedure for the student-counselor will be to begin immediately to listen to the client in terms of relationships. No matter what the client starts talking about, the counselor should know that eventually this must lead to relating to other people. I move the dialogue in this direction as soon as I am able, by means of questions, clarifications, or comments I direct to the client. This helps to focus the discussion quickly on the areas that I believe are paramount: "I am," "He/she is," "They are," and "Therefore." That is to say relationships are the "stuff" of counseling. Everything must be heard through this filter.

22

All relationship problems are related to either power or intimacy.

Since I have said in other contexts in this book that all therapeutic problems are relationship problems, I am now saying that all relationship problems are related to either power or intimacy. I am actually saying that *all the problems of therapy are related to power or intimacy.* I have to stretch a bit for this truism, but not a great deal. I have found that my clients are dealing either with (1) their sense of power, potency, worth, or self-esteem, or (2) their ability to love or to be vulnerable. These two variables are probably related. They may be the two sides of the same coin. But I find it easier to deal with them as two distinct issues, as I try to understand my client through all the data he or she is heaping on me.

Some readers may have already realized that what I have done is to agree with both Adler and Freud in the contention of what is the basis for human behavior. Adler believed that all behavior flows from a person's need to gain a sense of mastery and power to cope with the environment. Freud believed that all human behavior flows from the will to life and sexuality. I think they are both right. And if these two factors do indeed provide the bases of human behavior, then believing that all problems of therapy will be related to one or both of these bases is easy. Not surprisingly, I use these two "filter systems" to listen to my clients and to organize what they say.

23

The client's problem is rarely the real problem. What the client thinks is the problem is usually a bothersome symptom.

This truism has been repeatedly attacked by the public, by behavior therapists, by reality therapists, and by others. The reason this truism is still around is because so many of us doing therapy continually find it to be true. A client comes in to my office with the problem of continually being exploited by others. Now admittedly this is a sad state of affairs. As the client begins to give example after example of how people have been exploiting him, no doubt he or she is indeed being exploited. But if that is the problem, then why doesn't the person simply stop the exploitation. People don't generally exploit me. They probably don't generally exploit most of those reading this page. Why not? Perhaps the reason is because we know how to say "no." But the client has a vocabulary that includes the word "no." In many contexts the person uses the word "no" quite easily. Perhaps the reason is because we are able to see that a developing situation is not going to be a good one for us and we disengage from the situation. But most of my clients who complain of being exploited report that they, too, usually see that what is developing is not to their benefit, but they continued to allow it to develop. So what is the difference between the client who is constantly exploited and those of us who are not? In my experience as a therapist, the exploited individual is usually one of those who thinks of self as unworthy, not lovable, somehow not equal to others, and who believes that acceptance can not be gained unless others are allowed to exploit him or her. THAT IS THE PROBLEM. The client has been defining self as less than. . ., has been defining others as more than. . ., and with these two beliefs has concluded that the most appropriate set of behaviors is to permit others to exploit him or her. Actually exploitation is elicited from friends. Because of the client's own private, unconscious mythology about self, others, and how to live with these realities, the symptom is created that is believed to be the problem. But the real problem is mythology. Until that changes, the client's life will remain a painful one.

24

Mythology—the basis of it all.

As humans we apparently have always had fairy tales or myths that become a part of our culture and supply us with rules to live by. These myths or legends are found throughout the world in all cultures and are deemed to be a necessary part of what goes into the development of a culture. I am convinced that, in a similar fashion, each of us individually creates our own personal set of myths or guidelines of how to live our lives on a day-to-day basis. Like Alfred Adler I believe that very early in life, probably by the age of 6 or 7, we have come to believe general ideas about (1) ourselves (I'm clever, I'm stupid, I'm successful, I'm a klutz, etc., etc.); (2) the world (others) (people are helpful, people are trying to defeat me, people don't care unless you make them sorry, people are more worthy than I, people are to be used, etc., etc.); and with these two myths in place we then (3) develop some general guidelines of how to live with these truths. We develop a life style that generally is a consistent, reliable pattern of behaviors (avoid failure, make people the center of everything I do, get even, give in, make people laugh, be antagonistic, be charming, etc., etc). These three myths become the cornerstone of our existence, and they are the results of our life experiences for those first 6 or 7 years as children. They are what we believe is true because our *interpretation* of our experiences seems to indicate they are true. Once they are formulated in our young minds they become the solid, basic doctrines by which we live; they are generally unchallenged and unchanged for the rest of our lives; and then they are put into the unconscious.

As Adler has indicated in his writings, children are excellent observers of what goes on around them and to them, but unfortunately they are unsophisticated interpreters of these data. Often those myths they create for themselves are wrong, but they are the best they could do with their limited understanding. And they live out the rest of their lives following the logic of their unconscious mythology. Is there any wonder that so many people are living their lives in ways that are nonfunctional and painful!

25

New insight and new language give the client some wiggle room for a change.

I'm convinced that part of the reason why clients have not been able to "fix themselves" is because they are locked into a way of thinking about their problems. Also they are usually locked into a way of talking about their problems, both with others and with themselves. Giving the client a new way of speaking about and re-defining the situation can often work wonders. Illustrations are as follows:

"I don't want to" instead of "I can't."

"I am choosing" instead of "I have to."

"I'm not interested" instead of "I'm lazy."

"She doesn't like me" instead of "I'm no good."

"I'm slender" instead of "I'm skinny."

All of these are very simple examples of changing the language. If the language is changed, the issue is changing and the way one can think about the situation is changing, when that occurs, then an opportunity for solving the problem occurs.

26

The one who gives in gets even.

Some clients have such a sad tale to tell (if you'll let them). They have been so exploited! They are so badly used! They are so abused! And they are so prepared to tell about how others have "done them wrong." I can usually short-circuit this story by asking them how they get even. The client is almost startled by the question, but they can always answer it—usually with a smile. From this beginning I can point out to clients that in getting revenge they are demonstrating that they do have some power over their destiny. They are not merely victims that they believe themselves to be. They can and do affect things. I happen to think that this power can be used in better ways than getting even, and I say so. From this beginning we can start to develop new beliefs which will lead to new behaviors and will lead away from the life of victimization. Everyone has power enough to avoid being victimized. Getting even is evidence of this power. The trick is to put this power to better use.

27

Value-free counseling—it doesn't exist!

Values are very personal things. Most Americans today subscribe to the idea that no one should try to impose a value system on somebody else; a person's values are unique unto himself/herself and are almost sacred. Certainly, then, the counselor must guard against trying to influence the client's values. To do otherwise would be a great breach of ethics. . . . Nonsense! It can't be done!!

If values provide the rules by which we live our lives, and if how the client lives his or her life is what we are trying to change in counseling, then how can we counsel without overtly or covertly challenging our client's value system? This is a very tricky issue, not the simple myth that it might first appear.

Elsewhere in this book I have written that most counseling is either increasing or decreasing or otherwise modifying the client's superego. What is the super ego if it is not a value system? The "should's" and "should not's" of one's life are a part of every behavior that we adopt or decide against. It is the "stuff" of counseling. The argument might be put forth that challenging or exploring the client's value system is not the same as deliberately trying to influence the client's values. The key word in this argument is DELIBERATELY. Would having the counselor accidentally or unconsciously influence the client's value system be better? Research has shown conclusively that people are constantly influencing people, whether they are aware of it or not. Doing so really cannot be avoided. If two people are in the same room, they are bound to influence each other. And if values are the topic of discussion between them, influence will be exerted, deliberately or not. Research also has shown that client's values move in the direction of the counselor's values, as measured by pre- and post-values testing, when both the client and the counselor agree that counseling has been helpful. This is not true when the counseling is not seen as helpful. No indication was noted that the values were similar before counseling. This indicates that, deliberately or not, the counselor was affecting the client's value system.

If the counselor believes that a client should be less influenced by other people's needs or demands and should be more attuned to his or her own needs or wishes, that has to affect what the counselor is attempting to do in counseling—and this is dealing with values. If the counselor believes that mental health involves creating one's own life based upon the immediate circumstances, the counselor will provide a very different counseling experience than will a counselor who believes the good life is built upon the best that past experience has taught us. These are value systems! No such thing as "value-free counseling " exists. I want my students to realize this as they begin the practice of counseling.

28

Counseling is a process in which we try to avoid the win/lose part of living.

Many clients have spent their lives relating to others in terms of winning or losing, being right or wrong, being boss or servant, "getting" them, or "being had." These clients spend an incredible amount of energy defending themselves or attacking others—which of course is simply another kind of defense. They bring this view of life and this lifestyle into the counseling relationship, very often completely unaware that this is a major part of their existence. The counselor must be the one to avoid their trap of turning this relationship into a winner/loser event.

As a counselor, I do not want to defeat my client. If being a loser is part of the client's script, I certainly don't want to contribute to the delinquency of my client. But you can bet your last dollar, he will try to arrange things so that he loses. Losing is something with which such a client is familiar, is good at doing. In a twisted way, losing is such a client's way of winning. It probably gives him or her permission to get even, somehow. So I must be on my guard to see that the client is unable to do that to me.

Equally important is being able to avoid the client's defeating me—getting me into a one-upmanship show, being "right," "proving" something. These and other devices feed into such a client's neurosis. Focusing on the battle keeps us from focusing on the client. Whatever the client is "fighting" about is never as important as the fact that he or she *is* fighting—again. Believe it: the client will be looking for some reason where "attacking" is justified. If a reason can't be found, then a try will be made to create one. My responsibility as counselor is to see that the client doesn't do that to me.

In either case, the winning or the losing *is* the client's problem. The defeating or defeated script is keeping the client from being able to love or be loved (you can't do that with the enemy). Creating a climate in which winning or losing is an irrelevancy is a major step in the therapeutic process.

29

Never let a client "IT" on you.

Clients are generally unaware of how they are maintaining their problems. One of my jobs as the counselor is to help them become aware of what they are doing *or* help them become aware of how they keep themselves so unaware. This is more than a play on words. An important area of investigation is how clients manage to keep themselves in the dark so effectively. The way they use words is often one of their strategies.

We all know people who use words to cover up the truth as often as they uncover or reveal it. Usually they are deliberately and consciously using words to confuse a situation, either by lying or by leaving out important words or information. Clients often omits important information as they talk to the counselor. This is usually done unconsciously—but just as effectively as if it were conscious. Using the word "IT" a great deal is one way this is done.

> "*It's* not fair. . ." is not as clear a statement as "Steve is not fair."
>
> "*It* always happens. . ." is less definite than "Mom and Dad often do. . ."
>
> "That's just the way *it* is. . ." does not assign responsibility in the way that "Tom arranged for. . ."
>
> "*It* was an unpleasant situation" is really quite different from "I was being nasty."

In most cases, the word "it" is a substitute for naming "who" is doing "what." So when I find clients who often use the word "it," I immediately start training them to tell me "who and what" instead. A different way of talking leads to a different way of thinking which often leads to a different way of understanding: a primary goal of counseling.

SECTION III

CLIENTS' REASONS for COUNSELING

30

For many people, seeing a counselor is an admission that they have failed.

In another part of this book, I spoke of the need for a counselor to give the client hope. I wish to expand on that topic. I think a very important issue is for the student counselor to be aware that as a client enters the counseling office for the first time, the act of entering the office may be an admission of failure on the part of the client. The student counselor doesn't view the client in this way, of course. In fact, the student counselor is grateful that the client has come and is giving him or her the chance to develop counseling skills. The young counselor may have some apprehension about doing badly, but generally he or she is glad for the opportunity to work with a genuine client. This first meeting, for the counselor, is something he or she has been looking forward to doing. Not so for the client.

To many people, seeing a counselor or any mental health professional is seeing a "shrink" and that implies that the client is either "crazy" or too dumb to take care of his or her own life. Most people don't really understand that counseling deals largely with making unconscious material conscious, thereby giving the client a new opportunity to solve own problems with new, important data to consider. The client doesn't understand that the reason the problem hasn't been solved or resolved is that important unconscious material has been omitted from the problem-solving process. In the client's mind, he or she has looked at "all" the variables from "every" angle and hasn't been able to make things better. Soooo, the client thinks "I have failed"!

Feeling oneself a failure is the worst kind of discouragement. This is how a large percentage of counseling begins. Unless the student counselor is sensitive to this possibility the client may be lost within moments after the office door is closed—and the counselor may not know what went wrong. Giving your client hope, immediately, may spell the difference between the counselor's success or failure.

31

Sense of failure. . .

Discouragement is one of the biggest obstacles to a client's improvement in living life more satisfactorily. One of the biggest building blocks of discouragement is a sense of failure based upon true past experiences. You can't hide the fact that the client has indeed "goofed." So don't try to hide it! What I do instead is talk about a child learning to walk. All children trip, stumble, and fall when learning to walk. And they do it over and over again. But nobody says that have "failed" to walk; no one gives them an F grade in walking, and no one thinks they should stop trying to walk. We just encourage them to keep trying, they do keep trying, and eventually they walk successfully.

I want my clients to think of life as similar to walking. If I can help them see the similarity between themselves and the child learning to walk, they can find the courage to keep trying—to keep trying until they do it right. Giving the client a new way to talk about and think about life is one of the therapeutic tools I find helpful as a practitioner. I don't try to sugar-coat reality. But I do look for new ways to think about it as I work with my clients.

32

Clients usually hope you can help make things better without changing anything, at least as far as they're concerned.

With this client, and with most clients, only through the counselor's constant efforts to direct the focus to the client can the counselor hope to deal with the basic cause of difficulties. The client's saying that she realized she was the problem does *not* mean she really believed it; nor does it mean she wanted to work on herself to make things better. In fact, she tried to avoid it. That is why she needed a counselor who would not allow her to avoid what had to be made clear.

33

In their hearts they know they're not to blame.

One of my clients was a woman who had been married four times and had numerous lovers between and after these marriages. When she came in, she said she wanted to know what *she* was doing wrong, but she then tried to tell me about each of these men and what was wrong about them. She really did *not* appreciate that the only important common variable in all these relationships was herself, nor was she really prepared to examine her own lifestyle as the source of her difficulties. Occasionally she would say things like, "I know it's something that I'm doing wrong," but left to her own devices she would still focus on what was wrong with the men in her life and how they had "done her wrong." Constant effort on my part was needed to focus the sessions on her, on her lifestyle or script, or what she was hoping for or trying to avoid, on her beliefs about herself and about people—particularly men. These areas are where the problem lay. She knew it. But given her own choice of discussion, she would rather talk about "them." This situation is very similar to the moron who lost some money in the dark part of a city block but who insisted on looking for the money under the street light because to see was easier by the light, and also safer.

With this client, and with most clients, only through the counselor's constant efforts to direct the focus to the client can the counselor hope to deal with the basic causes of difficulties. The client's saying that she realized she was the problem does *not* mean she really believed it; nor does it mean she wanted to work on herself to make things better. In fact, she tried to avoid it. That is why she needed a counselor who would not allow her to avoid what had to be made clear.

34

The client secretly hopes that you too will fail. The the client won't look so stupid.

I have said in other places in this book that clients are clients because they have been unable to live their lives in a reasonably satisfying way. I also have stressed that clients' lack of success is not because they are too stupid to "do it right"; however, I firmly believe that they have not solved what is wrong in their lives. Very important data related to their problems are unconscious; and without the data no one can solve problems with which clients are living. Their intelligence has nothing to do with it.

But clients don't know that! For many clients the most difficult part about counseling is acknowledging that they need a counselor. For many, this amounts to admitting they aren't smart enough to solve what is wrong with their lives. With these kinds of clients, the counselor often is facing persons who feel humiliated and resentful of being in their situations. Clients often begin the relationship thinking: "What makes you so damn smart? Who do you think you are, anyway?" This isn't the entire picture, of course. Each client is hurting and wants help. Clients hope the counselor will help them. But they also secretly hope that the counselor will fail, thereby "proving" that nobody can resolve their situations, and the clients will save face. "See, even this co-called expert hasn't helped things—my failure is more acceptable."

I think a very important point for the student counselor is to be sensitive to this situation as the counseling relationship begins. A crucially necessary procedure is for clients to experience being treated with dignity and respect. Absolutely no trace of the counselor being "uppity" or condescending must exist or for any sign of being wishy-washy. The presence of the counselor must be that of quiet confidence, of one who expects to be treated with respect and will treat others in the same manner. From this stance the counseling can progress to the more advanced stages of the relationship. But the counseling process often begins with client hoping the counselor will fail—something the student counselor often fails to appreciate.

SECTION IV
COUNSELOR'S ROLE

35

One can do only what he thinks is the *right thing to do . . .* under the given circumstances.

No matter what the behavior may be, it is *always* the right thing to be doing—somehow. One of the jobs of therapy is to find out how what the client is doing (which often is cause for concern) is the right thing to be doing. How do you make sense of it? This can be done only by discovering the unconscious motives of the client—his or her unconscious intentions! When this is accomplished, the client can begin to reassess those intentions, reassess beliefs which are behind his or her intentions, and the process of therapy is well underway.

36

Responsibility: Creating one's life through choices. . .

For me, the essence of the "good life" is tightly interwoven with the concept of responsibility. In every case the good person living the good life is living a life characterized by responsibility. My definition of responsibility is creating one's life through conscious choices and then being accountable for those choices. I do not view responsibility as a heavy cross to bear. I do not think of responsibility as being in the control of others or living your life for others. On the contrary, I see the responsible person as the person who takes control of his or her own life to the greatest extent possible and is willing to stand by those choices both privately and publicly.

I also believe that the good person living the good life is concerned about others as well as self. I think the happy people I have known are, without exception, people who are committed to people and ideals beyond themselves. But I see this area of discussion as separate from that of responsibility; and I think that it is important to keep these concepts discrete, one from each other. They are related, to be sure, but they are discrete; and when my client and I discuss the "responsible life," I keep this distinction very much in focus. The first step toward mental health, in my opinion, is making conscious choices about life rather than responding in an automatic, habitual way or in allowing life to happen to you. Once responsibility is established we can then take a look at kinds of choices and their corresponding effects. But first we must learn to be responsible.

37

**To be intimate means to be vulnerable—
from a position of strength.**

The greatest thing we'll ever learn, as a song writer so aptly put it, is to learn how to love and be loved in return. Words of wisdom, to be sure, and I'm convinced that the single greatest obstacle to loving and being loved is the unwillingness to be vulnerable.

So many clients do not trust, and will not take the chance of truly being known. They live with an unconscious fear that if you really know them you won't like them. Therefore they must be guarded.

Other clients are afraid that unless they are the "boss" of a relationship they will be in a position of weakness. So they try to control a relationship and thereby negate the possibility of loving and being loved. Perhaps one of the greatest lessons a client learns in counseling is how to be vulnerable with a counselor and to discover it can be good—it can be safe. For many clients this may be the first step toward loving and being loved—the basis of mental health.

One of the greatest sins that a counselor can commit with a client is to exploit the client when they *are* vulnerable. This may well irrevocably teach a client never to be vulnerable again. This then may translate into never being able to love or be loved again. Being a good counselor carries with it some serious responsibilities.

38

You must train your client to be *your* client.

Although clients come to a counseling relationship with only a vague idea of what to expect, shortly after their arrival they will generally try to put the relationship into terms with which they are familiar. For them to try to do so is very reasonable. *And they must fail!!* The counseling relationship should be based primarily on terms decided upon by the counselor. What you talk about should be the result of the counselor's emphasis. Whether you ask questions or don't ask questions is the counselor's choice. If you do ask questions, the kind of questions you ask will have great impact upon what the client will narrate or think about. The counselor will decide to focus upon something or ignore it. How the client begins an interview and comes to expect things from an interview should be a reflection of the counselor's intentions, theories, and goals. The pacing, the rhythms, the tension or lack of it, the role the counselor will or will not play are all the responsibility of the counselor.

This may sound obvious, but the vast majority of student counselors come to beginning practicum with the idea that the client will lead, the counselor will follow, and something good will happen. Nonsense! Even Carl Rogers, the epitome of client-centered counseling, trained his clients to be client-centered clients. You will notice, if you listen to several tapes of Carl Rogers at work, that the voices and the specific content vary from client to client, but that Carl Rogers sounds the same; and eventually the sessions sound the same from client to client. Dr. Rogers may have been an unobtrusive teacher, but he certainly taught his clients to be *his* clients. So must we all.

39

I hold the counselor 75 to 80 percent responsible for what happens in a counseling interview.

As mentioned earlier, the counselor must train the client to be *his or her* client. To expand on the idea, I maintain that the client can do only what the counselor allows the person to do. This is a slight overstatement (I make them from time to time) but let me clarify.

If a client wants to talk about the unfairness of life, and I want to hear about who in particular is unfair and under what circumstances, then my questions and comments and interest should soon have the client telling me about whom and when. And if I'm not interested in unfairness, but am interested in the present relationship the client is having with his or her mother, then I can usually pursue this topic by the questions I ask, the comments I make, and the interest I display. In *no way* can a client continue to talk about "unfairness" if I am asking questions about and commenting upon the relationship with the mother. If I think a client is intellectualizing and rationalizing, and I want the client to get in touch with feelings, I merely change the focus by questions, comments, interest, or reflections to the experiencing of feelings. If I ask a client to stop talking and become aware of the clenching of his or her fists, the tension in jaw, and the apparent anger that is being felt at the moment, the focus of the session will go to feelings. I guarantee it! But if I ask the client to clarify a point in the story or argue with the client about the philosophy expressed, then I'll get more of that kind of dialogue. If a client wants to tell me about his or her past, and I want the person to focus on intentions, we will definitely follow my lead. No doubt about it! And I'm not suggesting that the counselor has to brutalize the client to get the counselor's way. All that has to be done is to ask the right questions, make the right comments, display the right interests, and it will happen. So the counselor is responsible for the interview. He or she is the professional and *should* be the responsible one.

40

The counselor, not the client, is in control of the interview— a fact that many beginners forget.

I often make suggestions to my students such as

"I'd like to see you ask about. . .,"

"It might be helpful if you don't let the client avoid. . .," or

"I suggest you focus on. . ."

The most frequent response I get from students is "I don't think this client is ready," or "I don't think this client will." Nonsense! As long as the client is willing to be the client and gives you permission to be the counselor, the counselor can choose to deal with any question at any time he or she wishes. This is not an overstatement. I realize that student counselors are more worried about losing clients than they will be later in their careers. But very few clients stop counseling because the counselor is doing his or her job well. If a particular issue seems important to deal with in the client's life, deal with it—NOW! You don't have to wait for the perfect moment or the "right time" to develop. When the counselor thinks the time is right, it *is* the right time. I used to believe that "timing" was a crucial issue in the counseling process. I don't any more. When I see that something is becoming obvious or important, I usually start dealing with it. I simply tell the client that I'd like him or her to tell me about. . .and the client will.

41

Give your clients hope. They need it.

By the time a client comes to see a counselor about a problem, he or she has probably tried to find help from friends and family first. Since the client is now in your counseling office, this means that the client and others were unsuccessful in solving the problem. The client is probably very discouraged by now, and often expects that you too will fail. After all, he or she isn't stupid; their friends aren't stupid; they have looked at this from every angle; and they failed to resolve the problem. "Maybe the problem is simply not solvable" goes through the minds of many clients as they begin to work with a counselor.

The counselor must be sensitive to this discouragement issue as the counseling relationship begins. Without promising a rose garden or pretending that I am infallible, I definitely try to give my clients reasons for hope, both directly and indirectly. Indirectly, I am confident of my ability as a counselor and it shows. I attempt to demonstrate my competence by getting the counseling process started soon in the first session. Directly, I may speak to the issue of discouragement, allowing the client to talk to the subject, and then make statements such as

> "I expect to be able to help you";
>
> "I know that you have gone through this before, but not with me, and I'm going to make a difference"; or
>
> "Well, I understand your reasons for discouragement, but I am good at what I do, so let's give this a try."

I don't care how other counselors do it, but I do stress the need for encouragement from time to time. I don't believe I have lost a client because of discouragement in many years. But it is a common reason for a client to quit.

42

If clients have made such a mess of things, how can they ever depend on themselves again.

As Alfred Adler mentioned in his early writing, a great problem which the counselor and client must overcome is the client's discouragement. Usually the client has been struggling with a problem for a long time before seeking counseling. The client probably has tried to solve the problem with friends and family before seeking counseling. Therefore, counseling often starts with a feeling of failure. Then, if the counselor does the job right, the focus of counseling turns to the client's unconscious intentions and beliefs so that it becomes increasingly clear that yes, indeed, the client is the reason for the difficulties. How easy for clients to conclude that they have made a mess of things and should never be trusted again! But they *must* be trusted again! They are all they have got!!

As the clients comes to realize that their present lives are ones of dissonance because those lives are a continuation of a life decided upon in childhood—as they come to realize that present beliefs about themselves and other people are a continuation of early beliefs about themselves and other people—as they come to appreciate that their present styles of living are adult versions of their childhood styles of living—what is imperative for them is to discover that these early decisions *were very good ones* for the times and places they believed existed. Those decisions and actions were the very best they could do under the circumstances in which they were living—as they understood them.

But clients also must appreciate that children often misinterpret circumstances in which they are living—not because they are stupid, but because they are children. As children, clients likely came to conclusions about themselves, people, the world, and how to live their lives based upon their childhood naive interpretation of things. And being normal, like the rest of us, they have been living their present adult lives based upon these myths of childhood, having consciously forgotten what they were. If their adult lifestyles are not working well, the reason is not because they are not smart enough to know how to live well. Rather, the reason is because they are still living by childhood myths which made sense at the time but which, in fact, may have been wrong; or, if they were correct at the time, they may be incorrect today.

A goal of counseling is to bring the unconscious memory to the conscious memory and to then examine yesterday's facts in today's light, with today's interpretation—the client's adult interpretation. In this process, I find that the client regains a sense of confidence and is quite willing and able to choose a new set of concepts about self, people, and the world and to develop a new style of living based upon these adult concepts.

Obviously, to accomplish the preceding the counselor will need to deal with the client's past as well as present life. I think those counselors who deal only in the here-and-now do the client as much a disservice as those counselors who deal primarily with the past. Only by dealing skillfully with both the past and present will the client be apt to have a better future.

43

Never contribute to the delinquency of your client.

I believe a person's life-style is a major reason for that person needing counseling. A slice of that life-style problem will inevitably be introduced into the counseling relationship. Freud called this transference. Whatever it is called, the counselor needs to recognize it for what it is and not fall into the trap of playing the expected script which the client wants from the counselor. A client who defines self as helpless can often elicit encouragement or support from the counselor—which the client will promptly sabotage. The critical client will often elicit explanation from the counselor which allows the client to argue with the counselor—which is why the client has so few friends. The flattering client is extremely effective in getting the counselor to "like" the client—which the client can then use to his or her own advantage in an unique way. The hostile client is so easy to dislike, thereby proving what the client knew already: This counselor is just like everyone else—"you gotta get the counselor before the counselor gets you." The list goes on and on. The counselor must be smart to recognize what the client is doing and must avoid reinforcing the client's behavior.

44

You must be willing to be responsible for making the client feel bad.

The vast majority of students who wish to become counselors or therapists are kindhearted people who do their best to avoid hurting others and who try to make the world a better place. I'm glad they are this kind of people. I like them. BUT these same students, almost by definition, have difficulty doing what is often a necessary part of the therapeutic process—being a part of what causes the client pain or anger or sadness. These negative feelings are what the client has been trying to avoid for a long time. The distortions, the denials, the projections—all of the defense mechanisms—have been used in order to avoid a certain truth and the bad feelings that will accompany that truth. If the counselor is successful, he or she will help clients to lower these defenses and allow the feared reality to enter their lives. When they do, they will finally be able to use the whole truth in living their lives. Only then will they be able to move beyond where they have been. But in the process they are apt to experience all the pain or anger or sadness which they have been avoiding. The counselor must be willing to be a part of the process that causes this pain. This is difficult for people who by nature are kind and caring—those who wish to be counselors. It is almost a paradox that the very characteristics which bring people into counseling are the same characteristics which often keep them from being successful. Along with being warm, kind, and caring must come a certain kind of toughness. Without this toughness the counselor will never really be good.

45

Clients are excellent at what they are doing wrong.

Make no mistake about it, your clients are experts at being themselves. And being themselves is where the trouble lies. Being themselves means living in a style that clients believe is the best way to live given the reality that clients believe is true—at both the conscious and unconscious levels of awareness. Clients are always themselves (they can't be otherwise), they practice and practice at it until they are experts at being themselves—long before they become clients and walk into your office.

By the time clients come to a counselor for help they are master players. They have rehearsed their roles until almost everything is on automatic, and they will try to keep it that way. Don't be surprised, therefore, if clients are able to successfully defend themselves from your initial attempts to bring about change. Like the horse who resists being led from a burning stable, your clients will resist being led from what they have always been. This is, of course, the actual goal of counseling.

46

Sincerity does not mean truth.

Clients generally are very sincere in what they say in counseling; they rarely deliberately lie. And yet I am always aware that what clients tells me may or may not be true. If clients believe something, they are going to behave as though it were true. At times, the counselor's primary task may be in helping clients re-think their truths; so paradoxically the counselor must be accepting of what clients say and still keep a modicum of skepticism handy and in the background.

47

You cannot *not* communicate.

Communication between people is as natural as life itself. It is one of the things humans do as part of their being human. We are always communicating—something—somehow. Unfortunately we don't always communicate well; we don't always communicate accurately; but we are always communicating.

Your clients are *always* communicating something to you—often more than they realize. They communicate with their words, with eyes, with body, with voice inflection, with unusual choice of words, with silence, with omissions, with emphasis, with forgetting, with slips, with smiles, and with tears. Usually they are using a combination of these. And the counselor's responsibility is to understand as much of the communication as possible. That is what you are trained to do. To the extent that you are able to take this communication and use it to your clients's advantage, to that extent will you be successful as a counselor.

48

Accepting one's humanness.

A surprising number of people literally suffer because they are only human. Somehow, sometime, they apparently bought the idea that if they really tried hard enough, they could be perfect and could make life perfect for others. "Perfect" is a strong word, and when faced with the word "perfect," everyone denies they feel guilty because they aren't perfect. But further dialogue usually reveals that somehow they *should* have been able to avoid mistakes or *should* have been able to resist temptation or *should* have been able to get along with Mr. X or *should* have been able to do it all, or *should* have been able to do whatever. And because they couldn't, they feel guilty. The only way they could have avoided this guilt feeling is if they had been more than they are. Usually this is finally translated as more nearly perfect.

I'm convinced that many clients are suffering from unnecessary feelings of guilt because they are still carrying around the admonitions and strictures they heard as children and they have not diluted them with the experiences of an adult. They accepted these "truths" in an unquestioning way (they were *good* kids, usually) and put them away into their unconscious intact, with all the *absolute* quality with which these "truths" are often directed toward children. Unchallenged, these absolutes now haunt them. Unchallenged, these absolutes trap the client with impossible expectations of self. Unwarranted guilt is the result.

Often, a goal of counseling may be as simple as helping the client develop realistic expectations of self—and others. So few absolutes exist!! People are not either honest or dishonest, diligent or lazy, courageous or cowardly. All of these characteristics—and most others—can be put on a continuum; few people fall at one end of the continuum or the other. Most of us fall somewhere in between. If I can help clients truly realize that indeed a continuum for a given characteristic exists and if I can then help clients find their place on the continuum, and find where they think the "normal" span is on the continuum, the chances are very high that we can dissipate unwarranted guilt feelings. I hope that my clients can sincerely say something like the following:

> "I'm reasonably OK—not perfect, but OK."
>
> "The chances are that you're OK—not perfect, but OK."
>
> "If the two of us work at it, there is a good chance we can live together in a OK fashion—not perfectly, but OK. Let's see what we can do. . ."

If I can help my clients reach this attitude about themselves and others, I think I will have been of real therapeutic service.

I want to make this perfectly clear. I am *not* advocating mediocrity. I *am* advocating judging ourselves and others on realistic bases and taking it from there.

49

The superego—you will either increase it or decrease it. Take your pick!

In the past, many of my colleagues were critical of the amount of time I spent teaching both Freud and Adler in my theories classes. But these two theorists provide the basis of all that I do as a counselor. I believe that the more recent therapies are merely modifications of Freud or Adler. Thoroughly understand these two theorists, discard some of each of them, and you have it. My trick is to find or create more modern forms of therapy based on these two theorists, but I am firmly grounded in their teachings.

The superego or social conscience is an important variable in any counseling whether the counselor thinks so or not. During the 1960s and early 1970s, many counselors were involved in helping their clients "discover themselves," "do their own thing," and become "self centered." Client centered therapy, Gestalt therapy, and Existentialism were all primarily involved with helping clients who had been overly socialized, overly conforming to the wishes of parents, or church, or other social systems. The therapeutic efforts were directed toward "self" and "I am-ness." Really, all of this was simply another way of talking about lessening the superego. Carl Rogers and Fritz Perls were using different terminology and different therapeutic models than Freudians were using. But they were concentrating on the superego, and they were trying to lessen it. Logotherapy, reality therapy, Christian therapy, Adlerian therapy were the therapies of the late 1970s, and their efforts were with clients who were undersocialized. These clients were so self-centered that they lacked the ability to love and merge themselves with others. They were lonely and yet seemed unable to commit themselves to something beyond themselves. The "me first" generation (which not surprisingly followed the period of Rogers, Perls, and company) needed the help of therapists to become more socialized, more a part of the greater social whole—a larger superego, if you will. Therapy seems to be either increasing or lessening the superego most of the time. I want my student counselors to realize that this is the case, to realize what they're doing and to do so in a professional and responsible manner.

50

Anger, fear, and sadness (or grief) are *always* that which the client is trying to avoid.

My life almost seems to be made up of threes—id, ego, and super ego; parent, adult, and child; body, mind, and spirit; water, fire, and air; the list goes on and on. Well, add one more threesome to the list—anger, fear, and sadness. This is the trinity of therapy. One or more of these emotions are always at the bottom line for the client. One or more of these emotions are what the client is trying to avoid. The psychological defense mechanisms are used to shield the clients from the feared realities that elicit these painful emotional responses. Getting through to these feared realities, experiencing these painful emotions, is the stuff of therapy.

Those students who are hoping for a career of happiness and joy are well advised to avoid a career in counseling. Counseling is about anger, fear, and sadness.

51

If you have to explain what counseling is to a client, you probably aren't doing much of it.

I rarely find myself in a position of explaining what counseling is to a client. My student counselors often find themselves in that position. I'm sure a number of factors contribute to this phenomenon, but one of them is obviously the fact that they *are* student counselors and they themselves may be asking the question: What is counseling, anyway? Not surprisingly, their clients ask their question for them. And then student counselors get bogged down in long, involved answers to that question.

Before practicum, all my student counselors have had one semester of personality theory and one semester of counseling theory. With all this, they still don't know what counseling is. How are they ever going to enlighten their client on the subject in the course of one session? And while the counselor is explaining about counseling, of course, counseling isn't being done. Neither client nor counselor are experiencing the counseling process—which is far more illustrative about counseling than any explanation ever will be.

If I *am* asked by a client to explain what counseling is all about, I generally answer in the following manner: "That's a reasonable question. . . .but I'd like to wait until the end of the session to answer it. Then I won't feel as rushed in answering, because I will have done some things that I hope to do in this first session."

This kind of counselor response generally satisfies the client at the moment. If I am as successful as I expect to be during the rest of the session, the answer to the question becomes self evident. Further explanation becomes unnecessary. If I'm not as successful at getting the counseling process underway as I had hoped, the question will come up again. In this case, I have a brief lecturette about counseling which I can insert; but when I'm doing it, I know I haven't been doing the counseling I'm talking about.

In any case, I think student counselors want to talk about counseling. Doing so is apparently easier and safer than dealing intimately with the client. Clients aren't the only ones who would rather intellectualize about counseling than do it.

People who cry too easily
are often covering up their anger.
People who anger too easily
are often covering up their tears.

So very often in counseling things are not the way they seem. Clients have devised a variety of ways of behaving that disguise the truth rather than show the truth. They do this unconsciously because at some level they believe that the real truth would be too difficult to live with, either for themselves, for others, or both. Freud recognized this phenomenon with his clients and labeled this disguising behavior as defense mechanisms. The counselor constantly must be alert for the use of defense mechanisms, avoid being misled by them, and help the client to stop living with them. The client cannot deal more effectively with life until the client starts living with the true world in a more honest fashion.

But clients are not deceiving or distorting reality in a conscious way. They really deceive themselves as successfully as they deceive those around them—perhaps even more so. And the counselor has the responsibility to recognize defense mechanisms and work through them. Doing so makes the counselor a different helper than the client's friends and neighbors. The untrained helper tries to deal with the obvious. When this is not enough, the trained counselor is the one who may help by hearing and seeing the unconscious truth, bringing this to the client's awareness, and giving him or her the opportunity to deal with a greater truth in a more honest way.

53

People who control their emotions may control more than they know.

A study done with drivers in Los Angeles who use the freeways is very relevant to a discussion of controlling emotions and repressing truth. What was discovered was that although experienced drivers described themselves as calm and confident as they entered the on-ramp of a freeway, instruments measuring heart rate, breathing, perspiration, and muscle tension indicated their bodies were in a state of near panic. These drivers were able to fool themselves into thinking that they weren't afraid of driving freeways (thus enabling them to function in an important way on a daily basis) but their bodies were not fooled; and their bodies were under great stress, whether as individuals each acknowledged it or not. Eventually their bodies would begin to evidence the long-term effect of stress and these drivers would not be able to understand why. They loved driving the freeways!

The same kind of phenomenon is happening to all of us all of the time. We are successful at denying on a conscious level those things in life we feel we must control in order to live our daily life. But denying them doesn't mean they don't exist. Nor does it mean that we aren't being affected by their existence. The job of the counselor is often similar to that of the instruments attached to drivers in the study mentioned above, i.e., to make the truth known, in spite of the drivers' denial that a truth exists.

54

At different times in a counseling relationship I believe the client and the counselor are in a kind of war.

This again is a bit of an overstatement, but I am trying to make a very important point which I think has been downplayed during the last 15 years of "humanistic" psychotherapy. During the reign of Carl Rogers and his followers at least an implicit (and often an explicit) idea prevailed that given a warm and accepting environment the client would automatically unfold into something beautiful, much like the unfolding of a rose—because it was Man's nature to do so! Ignored were the ideas of resistance, of defense mechanisms, of transference, of holding onto a life-style in spite of the penalties incurred, of the unconscious processes and motivation, of the belief systems as a basis for behavior. Instead the emphasis was on a neurosis which was the result of the conditioned positive regard of life. The cure for this neurosis was an environment of unconditional positive regard. This environment of unconditional positive regard, in and of itself, was thought to be all that the counselor or therapist had to offer the client in order for the client to improve.

I, of course, disagree with this position. Except for a few years in infancy, unconditional love and/or acceptance is not real. Once a person has knowledge and the capability of being held accountable, love and acceptance become conditional. This, in my opinion, is a normal fact of life. While I believe that indeed (1) the counselor must come to like the client and (2) the client must believe that the counselor is on his or her side, this by itself is not enough. So much more exists and at times the counseling relationship is a kind of war. But in this case the objective for the counselor is not to win the war; rather the counselor's objective is to keep the client from winning so that a new basis of living can be negotiated.

55

Do you want me to be a good counselor or a bad one?

I'm absolutely convinced that until clients are forced to take responsibility for making the above choice, out loud, many clients secretly hope I will be mediocre, at best—certainly not *too* successful. The resistance to change and improvement in their lives is an extremely important component of the counseling process, and I am afraid that most counselor-training programs do not prepare their students for it. So many student counselors are blind to the attempts of sabotage, denial, or avoidance in which the client is involved. A scene that I see repeated over and over again goes something like this:

Co: I have noticed that you never mention your family relationships.

Cl: I was afraid that you were going to ask about that. I really don't want to talk about my family right now. I just get too upset.

Co: OK. What do you want to talk about?. . .

Variations on this theme occur far too frequently for it to be accidental or coincidental. Resistance this blatant must be dealt with and overcome or the counseling relationship is doomed to be fruitless. One way I suggest that this scene be handled is for the counselor to ask this question and insist upon an answer:

Co: Do you want me to be a good counselor or a bad one?

Cl: Uhmm-a good one, naturally. But I just don't like talking about my family—at least not right now.

Co: Well, if I am to do a good job, I think we should begin dealing with family right now.

Nine times out of ten, clients will sigh a sigh of relief and begin dealing with a subject that they *know* they have been avoiding. The other 10 percent of the time, they may continue their resistance. If they do, I may simply drop the subject—especially if this is the first time we have gone through this scene. By the third time, however, we deal with either the topic in question or the issue of power and control that has obviously developed in the counseling relationship. More about this in another section of this book.

SECTION V
PROBLEMS in COUNSELING

56

Problems of counseling: Some are solved, others are resolved.

As I have mentioned in another part of this book, what the client brings in as the problem rarely is the problem with which we will be working. But sooner or later the problem will come into focus. Most people believe that once you discover the problem, you then logically set about solving it. You make new choices, you decide to do this instead of that, you change your goals or methods for obtaining those goals, and/or you deliberately and consciously do something to solve the problem. And at times you indeed do just that.

However, sometimes what occurs is a resolution of rather than a solution to a problem. At times merely seeing or misunderstanding an event or a situation in a new, undistorted way in-and-of-itself resolves the problem. Nothing new is decided upon. No actions are planned or carried out. Suddenly, with a new understanding, the problem dissolves, the pain is gone, the anger is dissipated, the client is at peace—and nothing consciously takes place.

Realizing that both resolution and solution are possible outcomes of counseling is important for the beginning counselor. It helps explain why both Carl Rogers and William Glasser both have claimed success on such different bases. They are both right. Rogers often was dealing with resolution of a problem; Glasser often was dealing with solution to a problem. They both are valid. I think it best for the counselor to be prepared to deal with both of them.

57

What they have done to others they will do to you—somehow.

Since I believe that some aspect of the client's style of living is the trigger for discontent, I give great importance to analyzing the client's style of interaction with me in the counseling sessions. I assume that sooner or later (usually sooner) the client will demonstrate one part of his or her style of living. My responsibility is to recognize this when it happens. Also I have the responsibility to respond to this style in a therapeutic manner rather than in the manner that the client is anticipating.

Example: As a child, a girl may have learned to get along in life by being cute and cuddly. This life-style can be successful for a long time. Many men enjoy dating or being with a "cute" woman. But usually by the time a woman is in her 30s or 40s, being cute doesn't work anymore. And being cute is her only way of behaving—especially with men. Being cute is no longer functional; she begins to be less successful in her relationships and finally comes to counseling to find out what is wrong. I *know* this woman will be cute with me in the counseling relationship. "Being cute" is where the therapy will begin.

Other clients will bring other styles by which they live their lives: humorous, seductive, belligerent, helpless, irresponsible, and many others. They will, each of them, try to use their style of living on me. They have to! I will have the best situation possible to help them therapeutically.

This concept is very similar to the Freudian concept of transference. Freud was right about the importance of this phenonmenon. I think that perhaps I have enlarged upon it. But as you see a pattern of behavior developing in your client's dialogue, rest assured that that pattern will be a part of the client-counselor relationship in the not-too-distant future. Be prepared to use it as a major therapeutic tool.

58

Counseling ultimately deals with anger or fear or sadness. It is not a happy business.

As a counselor educator I find that the majority of people who want to be counselors are those who like people, want to help people, and want people to like them. The counseling student typically enjoys human relationships and sees counseling as an opportunity to make a living enjoying people who are enjoying them. A successful counselor "ain't that"!!

Counseling is not being paid for being friendly. On the contrary, counseling is being paid to help people do what they consciously don't want to do, and what they have been successful at avoiding. Clients, for the most part, do not enjoy working with their counselor. If the counselor is doing a good job, he or she is taking clients into areas of themselves they do not want to know about. Sooner or later the client is going to be experiencing that which he or she has been defending against; and it always involves the negative feelings of anger, sadness, or fear. ALWAYS!!

With many clients a honeymoon period does exist as you begin counseling. Moving toward a unique, intimate relationship can be pleasant. But once you move beyond the honeymoon—which should *not* last very long—the work, the struggle, and the negative "stuff" begin. This part of the counseling relationship is what lasts the longest. This is how the counselor spends the majority of the counseling time. Once clients begin to feel good about themselves and their own lives, the time together is almost over. Clients don't continue coming to counseling when things are going well for them. They have better ways to spend their money.

So the result is that brief periods, at the beginning and end of a counseling relationship, are pleasant. They probably represent a total of less than 20 percent of the relationship. If having people like you is an important part of your life-style, then the possibility is highly likely that being a good counselor is not your cup of tea. Anger, fear, and sadness comprise the greater part of counseling, not sunshine and roses.

59

Misunderstanding the counselor is a great defense for the client.

I want students to realize that clients originally will view the counselor in the same way they view people in general and will respond to the counselor in their typical fashion, i.e., their style of living. Therefore, the probability is very high that early in the relationship many clients will unconsciously but very deliberately misunderstand or misinterpret the counselor in some way. Don't be surprised and don't be angry. They are simply doing what comes naturally, i.e., distorting things to make them fit what they want to believe, protecting their view of the truth, justifying themselves and their behavior, and generally putting the counselor into the mold of the rest of "them" who have been giving the clients trouble.

The counselor should be prepared for this to happen and hope to be able to use the situation to help clients see what they did, how they did it, how and where they have done this with other people, and how this misunderstanding is a show of their life-style. But above all, the counselor should not feel guilty or inept. I have watched student counselors be very explicit, very clear, very accurate with their clients and still be misunderstood. The client had to work at misunderstanding the counselor, which is exactly what the client was doing, but the student counselor accepted responsibility for the problem, which is what the client was hoping would happen—and a good opportunity for a therapeutic intervention had slipped by.

60

Too logical or too intuitive? That is the question!

I believe that the counseling of the 1960s and early 1970s was successful with clients who had come to rely too much on their left brain to cope with daily living. They were too logical, too sequential, too much involved with cause and effect relationships, too linear in their thinking. The right side of their brain had atrophied, and they were not experiencing life nor dealing with life with an intuitive, wholistic, romantic thinking. Many clients of the 1960s literally could not see the forest because they were too busy studying the individual trees. Their therapy reawakened the right brain. They began to see the world in a more global, nonlinear, less logical, more emotional way. They, in effect, added an entirely new dimension to their lives. By adding the right-brain responses to the left brain responses, the client was able to deal with life in a more balanced way—in a more satisfying way.

I believe that successful therapy of the late 1970s and early 1980s dealt with many clients who were the counterparts to the earlier era. These clients have come to rely too heavily on the right brain. Many of these clients are nonlogical in the way they are living their lives. They fail to see the individual trees that make up the forest, and as a result they fail to appreciate the cause and effect aspects of life. They are so spontaneous they are living from one crisis to the next, with little or no idea of how to break the crisis cycle. For these clients the type of therapy of the 1960s and 1970s might be a disaster. These clients need to stimulate the left brain and add the linear dimension to their lives in order to achieve a better balance for living.

One of the decisions I have to make in the counseling relationship is whether to emphasize right or left brain therapy. Actually, I may do both at different stages of the relationship. But I think an important aspect is for the counselor to be sensitive to this issue, to choose the appropriate modality of counseling for the individual client, and to know when he or she is doing what along this continuum of linear and nonlinear counseling.

61

Clients are never "stuck" in their counseling—they are hanging on.

From time to time I hear my students, and indeed even some colleagues, talk about their clients being "stuck," being unable to move in the counseling process, being at an "impasse" in their therapy. And apparently the counselor and the client are both waiting and hoping to be unstuck and through the impasse—somehow. The "somehow" is usually more of whatever they have been doing up to this point. I don't believe they are stuck; I believe they are holding on to their position, either because they are afraid to risk a new position or because their "stuck" point is a good point for their yet unconscious intention. In either case, more-of-the-same is not in order (even it it is louder and slower). I am likely to assume that unconscious motivation still needs to be discovered. When this is discovered, clients will let go of their old positions and take new, more appropriate stances toward the therapeutic process. So I do not merely hope the client will become unstuck; I work at finding good reasons for the client to let go.

62

Who's holding back—the counselor or client ?

Generally the agreement is that if the content of a session seems to go no where or appears to go in circles, the reason is because the client is resisting the therapeutic process or is avoiding a particular area of dissonance. The client is judged as not wanting to "get on with it." Without question, this is often true. But what also is often true is that the *counselor* is avoiding the next step, or the strong feeling, or the next part of the process. This counselor-avoidance is usually pre-conscious; but it is just as important as client resistance and must be constantly guarded against. The client will go no farther than the counselor is willing to go. The client only can go as close to strong feelings as the counselor is willing to go. If I see my student counselors going in circles with their clients, my first reaction is to watch counseling process to see if the counselor is contributing to the problem. Oftentimes this is the case!

63

Depression: Is it anger, sadness or despair?

Many clients come to counseling with the self-diagnosis that they are depressed. They don't really know what that means, but they are feeling very low. Three kinds of depression exist. One kind of depression is suppressed anger turned against oneself. Another kind of depression occurs in many people who say they are depressed and are very sad because of great loss or grief. The third kind occurs in others who say they are depressed but are really in a state of great despair and discouragement. One of my early counseling attempts when working with a "depressed" client is to find out with which of these three depressions the client is living.

Symptoms of these three kinds of depression appear to be very similar, but I believe that the only type I can work with, without the aid of drugs, is that stemming from suppressed anger which the client is turning against self. The other forms of depression, in my opinion, can best be treated in conjunction with drug therapies. For me, that means referring the client to a psychiatrist, or cooperating with a psychiatrist in my treatment. I do *not* believe that drug therapy, without dealing with other aspects of the client's life, is enough. But I also am convinced that *only* talk therapy is equally insufficient for these clients. a need exists for mood altering drugs to get clients to a level where talking and acting are possible.

Because most depressed clients come into my office looking the same, I cannot tell immediately with which kind of depression I'm dealing. I begin looking for areas of hostility in their lives of which they may be unaware. If I don't find any with the first 8 to 10 visits, I soon will consult with a psychiatrist with whom I have a working relationship or refer the client to one of several psychiatrists in whom I have some trust. Most of my depressed clients indeed are angry, and they are denying it, consciously; so I am very comfortable in working with them. But for those whom I see who really are extremely sad or in a state of despair, some other course of action is called for.

64

Resentment—of whom?

Unless a client is unusually neurotic, they (like us) do not hold on to hidden resentments in an abstract manner or about abstract situations. Almost without exception, if individuals continue to be resentful about something they are resentful about some*one*. As a counselor I try to put the focus on the one at whom the resentment is directed; many clients have been denying the "whom" and have been vaguely aware of the "what" of their resentment. This is a part of what Fritz Perls called "unfinished business." As indicated in another section of this book, I believe that all counseling almost always relates to relationships. I therefore believe that becoming aware of repressed resentment toward a particular individual is an important component of counseling, and I actively search out specific resentments with my clients.

When a repressed resentment is brought to awareness and when that resentment is tied to a particular person, we are then in a good position to examine the relationship of the client and the other in a more reasonable, contemporary light. Of particular importance in this examination is the client's role in the relationship, expectations, and demands. Like the resentment, these too have often been repressed and so have been influencing the client without the client's awareness.

I have no interest in the catharsis of anger or resentment for its own sake, as do some counselors. If catharsis has any value at all, I believe it is getting the client in touch with more truthful and more complete understanding of a relationship that has been and continues to be significant to the client. With this better understanding the client will have a better chance to put this relationship on a constructive basis and get on with his or her life in a more satisfying way.

SECTION VI
TECHNIQUES and PROCEDURES

65

There's no such thing as nothing.

In another section of this book I mention asking the clients what they are thinking and finding it usually important. I must say, however, that many clients do not always want to share what they are thinking or may not be aware of what they are thinking. In either case, clients will often answer the question, "What are you thinking?" with answers such as:

"Nothing. . . ."

"I don't know. . . ."

"Actually my mind is a blank right now. . . ."

"I wasn't thinking anything. . . ."

The beginning counselor may believe the client and not pursue the issue. Usually to do so is a mistake.

For clients not to be thinking *something* is impossible. The mind is always functioning; it is always thinking. Even when we sleep, we think. Our thoughts may not be sequential; they may not seem to be logical; they may not seem to fit the present conversation. So clients may not feel comfortable in sharing their thoughts at any given moment. That's fine. And I may choose to allow them to avoid telling me what they are thinking—but not because I believe that their minds are blank. My choice of whether to pursue an issue will be influenced by many factors, but believing clients who say they are not thinking of anything is not one of them. I don't want my students to believe it, either. The client cannot not think, and don't forget that.

66

**Don't listen to the client's story.
Listen for their life-style within the story.**

Clients generally expect to tell you what their problems are and then why they have these problems—and this gives them license to tell you the story of their lives. In my experience their story is usually a justification of why they are as they are, and "the problem" is usually someone else's fault. Some clients are more subtle about this formulation than others, but the bottom line is usually, "Ain't it awful and what else could I do?"

The client has told this story many times before they see a counselor, and they usually have it well rehearsed. They also can usually make the story interesting. But "the story" is usually irrelevant—at least in terms which the client emphasizes. If you must listen to a client's story, then use the story to ascertain patterns of the client's behavior (not all the others in the cast of characters). If you can begin to see patterns of the client's behavior in the relationships, you may be able to move in on the client's life-style and the mythology behind the life-style. This will happen only if you listen to your client within a certain context. Otherwise, the "story" is usually a waste of time and money—although I know a great many counselors who make a good living doing just that: wasting their client's time and money.

67

Client history: On my terms only!

Clients enter counseling expecting to tell the counselor about their life histories. Unfortunately, many counselors expect to listen to it—and do! And they listen to the client's history on the client's terms, in the client's way, with the client's emphasis. Listening to the story is an easy way for the counselor to earn money, but I'm convinced that it rarely benefits the client. The client's history does have a place in counseling, but not as a central focus of the process—and certainly not in the format which the client is likely to use.

When I consider the client's history, it is not to look for causes of present behavior or present difficulties. Present behaviors or present relationships are the result of present choices based upon present perceptions and present belief systems. Changes can only take place in the present. The present is where the primary focus of the counseling process must be. When I begin to find things in the client's present life that lead to certain hunches on my part about their unconscious beliefs, I may then look to their past to find similar patterns of behavior or similar situations to see if indeed a history exists of doing things in a certain way that is *consistent*. If we find such a consistency, we can explore what seems to be supporting it. And at times, examining a constant pattern of behavior over a long period of time can be less threatening to the client and raise less resistance and defensiveness. But we go to the client's past only when I am looking for something very specific, and it is always directly related to something in the client's present life: an early memory, the relationship with Mom or Dad, interactions with siblings, early success experiences and early failures—all dealing with early definitions of self, of people, of love or trust, or of life in general.

Usually we find that, given the client's perceptions of the reality of an early period, definitions of self, people, and/or life were very reasonable. They made sense. And perhaps the difficulties the client is having today stem from maintaining those early definitions when they no longer are appropriate or valid. Often the client constructs these early definitions of self or others, never questions them again, and lives his or her life seeing the world and dealing with it through these lenses. So using history to understand the present can be very helpful; but the emphasis must be on the here and now. The counselor's responsibility is to keep it there and use the past only when necessary and in a very precise way.

68

Patterns of behavior, early memories, familiar situations—all can be keys to early intentionality.

When I do allow the client to narrate material or to tell me "the story" I try to find similar patterns of behavior at different parts of "the story" and I ask the client to help me make sense of the apparent pattern. Inevitably we can begin to see how the pattern has been used in different situations in the same way; the intentionality of such behavior often becomes evident. So, too, for early memories of a current event or situation in the client's life. If something is of real significance in the client's present life, I often ask the client if something is vaguely familiar about the situation; does he or she have any early memories of a similar event in younger life? If the answer is yes, we can often explore these early memories (which are often safely distant and less threatening than the present) and then we can find greater meaning to the current events in the client's life.

This is the way I use history. I find something significant in the present, find its counterpart in the client's past, bring together this past and present, and help the client discover how he or she is using this particular situation in creating his or her life. . .again!

69

Your insight is good.
Your client's developing that insight is better.

After you have been a counselor for a while, and if you have been reasonably good at it, you will start seeing the dynamics of your client; you will start seeing the real problem of your client long, long before your client does. Student counselors are usually amazed at how quickly I can describe each client, the client's life-style, and the probable area of discontent in the client's life. Often I can do so in minutes.

But although the ability to gain this insight is important, the ability to help your client gain this insight is much more important. This second ability is the ultimate goal of the student counselor. . .and the much more difficult to accomplish.

70

Transference: When it happens, you've struck gold! Go for it!

The client's problem is *always* the script they have developed and relied upon to deal with life and with people. Sooner or later the client will start doing to the counselor that part of their script that creates the difficulty in the client's life. It is bound to happen; and when it does, the counselor has the golden chance. Calling attention to the dynamics occurring in the office at that very moment and examining the client's assumptions underlying the behavior which *just happened* (not something the client has been telling you happened with somebody else) is an extremely powerful experience. If the counselor can step outside the normal reaction to the client and what the client is doing to the counselor and ask the client to examine what the client is doing or trying to do—not as a challenge but as a professional, examining the data—the client's troublesome script becomes the focus of the interview. Finally! Finally you can deal directly with what the client perceives, believes, and acts upon. You can question what the client hopes or expects will happen, what effect the client actually is having on the counselor, and how the client's script is working against him or her. It is a wonderful therapeutic moment.

One experience of this kind will not induce a great change in the client's life-style. But a number of these experiences will begin to weaken the clients' resistance to change, will direct the clients' attention to themselves rather than others when things start going badly, and true change in life-style becomes a real possibility.

To illustrate how important I think capitalizing upon the actual interaction between client and counselor can be, I suggest that one such experience is worth ten of anything else that can take place during the counseling interview—at least ten!

71

Catharsis doesn't cure anything; but it may be a step toward curing.

Some counselors believe that catharsis, in and of itself, is a good thing. They believe the expression of a strong feeling such as rage or grief or fear unlocks a curative power in the individual. Believing this, a great deal of time and energy is spent in therapy trying to get the client to express these strong feelings, over and over again, until the bad feeling is used up and the client feels good again.

I don't agree with this position at all. In my experience, people can go for years expressing "the feeling" and never seem to get over it. In fact, the more they express their rage or grief, the better they seem to become in expressing it (they can cathart on a moment's notice) and the less good it seems to do. They are less at ease at the end of each catharsis. I believe this is so because the focus is placed on expressing and experiencing the rage or grief itself, rather than to that which feelings are attached.

I believe that people do indeed try to avoid bad feelings. I believe that people resort to using defense mechanisms in order to avoid perceiving, thinking, or believing something is true, because these perceptions, thoughts, or beliefs trigger very unpleasant feelings. But the perceptions, or thoughts or beliefs are important. Feelings they trigger are only reactions to thoughts or beliefs. These perceptions, thoughts, or beliefs must be explored, analyzed, and re-assessed, not the feelings that follow them. Feelings are the natural response to what we believe is true. One doesn't change a natural response to a situation. One *may* change the *meaning* they give to a situation; this in turn will change the emotional response to the situation. But changing the meaning we attach to a reality is important. Feelings reflect the meaning of the situation, not the situation itself.

So, when my clients finally stop avoiding the truth and stop avoiding the feeling of rage or pain that accompanies the truth, I allow them time to allow the great passion to pass. Then I focus on material that triggered the strong feelings, not the feelings themselves. Now that the client has stopped avoiding the painful feelings, we can finally get to the material that triggers the pain. This is the stuff of therapeutic change. This is where I spend my efforts.

In summary, then, catharsis is important, but only to the extent that it allows the client and me to get to material that is triggering the painful feelings the client has been successfully avoiding. After catharsis, a new stage of therapy begins.

72

I actually throw a "counselor switch" on and off at will.

As students hear me discuss the counseling process, see me demonstrate counseling, and describe client behavior—motivation, life-style, myths, etc.—they often ask if I can still enjoy friends, love my wife, and be comfortable with people in general. Definitely! A gynecologist is able to go home and enjoy sex with his or her spouse! So, too, can the counselor leave the office and be "one of the guys or gals."

Of course, the g-y-n would be more likely to notice something wrong with the spouse's reproductive organs than the typical person. So, too, the counselor will never again be able to see people through the naive eyes of the layman. But counseling is, for me, a definite set of responsibilities, permissions, and expectations that I don't accept unless I choose to. When I do choose to be a counselor, I throw a switch; I begin to focus my attention and my energy in a very special way; and I behave accordingly. My "style" of counseling is *very* different from my "style" of teaching or being a friend. I am genuine in all these situations. But how I am is definitely a reflection of what the situation calls for. I don't throw the counseling switch unless I want to.

73

The best basis for establishing the counseling relationship is that of the counselor's competence, not of being friendly.

As I view student counselors during their early sessions with clients, I watch them time and time again fail to pick up on the client's body language or choice of words, or fail to ask an obvious question. When I later suggest they should have done so, I'm inevitably told they were trying to establish a counseling relationship before getting into "that stuff." This usually translates into helping the client feel comfortable with the counselor, which further translates into the counselor being friendly with the client.

I am firmly convinced that the client should experience the counseling process during the first interview. I, myself, try to begin the counseling process as soon as possible—within the first 5 to 10 minutes if I am able. I believe that the best way to establish the counseling relationship is by demonstrating my competence as a counselor. Being a nice guy and doing the stuff of counseling are not mutually exclusive. Of course I want clients to feel that they can trust me and put themselves in my professional hands. I don't advocate being pushy, nasty, or rude later in the relationship, either. I try to be the same in the first interview as I am in the rest of the counseling sessions, and I start counseling as soon as possible.

I am seldom the first person the client comes to for help with their problem. They have first talked with friends, parents, or priests. I want them to know, as quickly as is possible, that working with me will be different than talking to friends, which hadn't been helpful. Doing my "counseling stuff" is the best way for them to know that, so I start counseling immediately. if clients have experienced the counseling process during the first interview, they will know it; they will know that it is something different than they have experienced with friends and neighbors; and they will be back. Client comfort is not what I strive for in establishing a counseling relationship. Client's confidence in me as a counselor is.

74

Beginning the interview.

I am always amazed and amused at the difficulty many student counselors starting the interview, particularly the first interview. I generally suggest they try the obvious:

> "Why don't you begin."
>
> "Where would you like to begin?"
>
> "Why did you come to see me?"
>
> "Why did you come to counseling?"
>
> "How would you like to start?"

All of these questions are very broad, nondirective questions, in one sense; in another sense they are very specific and very directive. They all give the client great freedom to pick a starting place, and they seem to put the client in control. But they do more. They really instruct the client that I am making him or her responsible for starting. I, therefore, am in charge of the interview, since I am deciding who starts. By creating a somewhat ambiguous situation, I can observe how the client responds in order to put self in a position where he or she is more secure—a slice of the client's life-style. With this kind of opening, I am preventing the client from making me responsible for finding the right thing to talk about. If I am made responsible for finding the "right" topic I can easily be made to fail—which many clients are accustomed to doing to others, especially authority figures. With this kind of opening, I don't give the client clues as to what I am interested in hearing, so they can neither please me, entertain me, nor counterpunch me. With this kind of beginning, having minimal direction from me, I am able to observe who and what the client wants me to know about (and, indirectly, who is omitted that one might expect to be included).

All of this from an apparently relaxed, nondirective opening question asked by a counselor who is apparently waiting to begin.

75

Beginning the relationship.

To realize that a person is always giving off clues about who they are as a person is very important; they are always behaving. For me as a counselor, the very first moment I see my clients is when I start working. How they first make eye contact, how they rise from their chair, how they greet me, what they do after they say hello, how they enter my office, all of these things and many more are all indicators about persons and their life-style. I immediately begin to process this information. I know it will be important to what we will be doing in the counseling relationship.

For my part, I try to greet my client with a gentle smile; I say "Hello, I'm Jim Carnevale, and I assume that you are . . . . Let's go to my office, shall we?" I don't shake hands unless they initiate it, and I don't do much in the way of small talk—especially on the first interview. I don't initiate shaking hands because I don't push myself into their space at the first opportunity. I don't start small-talking because I don't want to teach them that small talk is part of my expectation. This is going to be a different kind of relationship than they have had with their friends and neighbors, so I don't want to start it in the way friends and neighbors do.

When we get to my office I give them a moment to look at the surroundings and become accustomed to the room. All the chairs in my office are identical, so I let them pick their chairs; then I choose mine (four rolling armchairs are in my office). I then ask them where they would like to begin. I try to ask them to begin before they have a chance to ask me, "How shall I begin?" or "How do we get started?" I do not want them to give me the responsibility of finding the right topic for the interview—my chances of failing are too high and I will be put in the position of trying harder. At times I'm not fast enough to avoid this question (when that occurs I assume those clients are fast at shifting responsibility), so I usually answer with something like, "Probably you should begin by telling me about those areas of your life that are giving you difficulty." This is a broad assignment. They are still responsible for beginning and they usually do.

With this kind of opening, I have taught my clients that I will not make things easy for them, that I am in charge, and that I expect to respond to them, not them to me, as this relationship begins. I have not given them many clues about myself so they can't jump to conclusions about me. Nor do they have many clues about how they "should be" in their half of the relationship. I don't want them picking up the other half of my script. I want them to reveal *their* script to me.

I *never* say anything that even faintly resembles, "We can talk about anything you want to talk about." I don't want them getting started by talking about the San Diego Chargers or the weather, or the big sale on sheets at the Broadway. I want them to focus on themselves, on their life, on the dissonance, so that is where I want them to begin.

76

. . . and you?

If one thing characterizes the talk of clients in the early stages of counseling, it is their tendency to talk about other people and how those others are somehow involved in their problems. Comments by the client about the client are apt to be minimal, unless the counselor works at focusing the dialogue upon the client. I have found that attaching the question "and you?" to the end of the client's comments about others is a very painless way to keep the focus of the client. After adding a couple of "and you's" to the client's comments about others, the client will quickly learn what you are after and where the focus of interest lies.

77

I hate the question, "How do you feel?" or "How are you feeling?"

In part, I dislike the "feeling" questions because I have heard them so many thousands of times. Many, many student counselors come to practicum expecting to ask a "feeling" question. They also seem to expect great things to happen when the question is answered. They are generally disappointed.

The major reason I dislike "feeling" questions is that the answers the clients give to them are either not helpful or have little to do with feelings. "I feel he shouldn't have done that" is not a feeling; it is a thought. "I feel he is trying to hurt me, so I'm going to hurt him first" is not a feeling; it is a thought. "I feel I can trust her" is also a thought. "I feel angry" is indeed a feeling; but if the client is really feeling angry and I have to ask what he or she is feeling, the client usually wonder, whether or not I am paying attention.

The number of feelings we can have are very few. We can be happy, sad, disappointed, angry, fearful, or contented. That's about it! And we are unable to speak of these feelings in ways that easily discriminate the degree of the feeling—they are very global descriptions. I think that far more effective questions are the following:

> "What are you experiencing right now?"
>
> "And how do you respond to that?"
>
> "What kind of reaction do you have to that?"

These questions ask the client to focus on self and direct him or her to be aware of what is occurring (feeling, thinking, behaving). Generally the client will report on all of the above which is usually more helpful and easier to respond to than is the question, "How are you feeling?"

Most of the time, when clients say "I feel that's not fair," they are talking about thinking in the right hemisphere of the brain, the intuitive rather than the logical hemisphere of the brain. We respond to our world from both hemispheres of the brain. We think in both logical, sequential, cause/effect ways and in nonlogical, wholistic ways. But they are both ways of thinking. I believe that when most counselors ask someone how they feel, they are really asking them to become aware of how they are responding from the intuitive, wholistic part of the brain. I think *my* questions are a better way to do that.

78

I always have three Here/Nows from which to choose.

Student counselors seem to have difficulty moving the Here and Now. I tell them that it might be easier if they think of having three separate Here and Nows from which to choose

1. The counselor's Here and Now.
2. The client's Here and Now.
3. The client and counselor's Here and Now.

1. The counselor's Here and Now is usually the easiest choice. Most student-counselors can confidently say, "At this moment I am feeling/thinking/wondering/wanting to respond to you. . . ." They can usually tune into themselves in the immediate moment and share that with the client.

2. The client's Here and Now can often be brought into focus by asking the client about his or her immediate perceptions, or feelings or thoughts. Clients often can be helped by calling attention to their body language and asking them to give it meaning in terms of feelings, thoughts, or beliefs.

3. Our Here and Now (counselor/client's) usually call attention to the interactions taking place between the client and counselor, e.g., "I notice that we are sitting here and sparring with each other. Do you experience us in this way?"

Any one of these three Here and Nows can prove to be productive. I believe the most productive is the client's; the second best is ours; the least productive, but also the easiest, is the counselor's. At any moment the counselor can shift to one of them. They don't have to wait for a magic moment.

79

By-Pass the client's defenses.

In another part of this book I have written about the advantage of non-rehearsed dialogue as a means of lowering or avoiding the defense mechanisms which the client is apt to use in normal conversation. Working with body language is one way of doing this. Asking questions which generate un-normal material is another. Illustrations of such questions are as follows:

> "If you were an animal, what kind of animal would you be?"
>
> "If you were a building, what kind of building would you be? what kind of exterior? Interior? Furnishings?"
>
> "If an artist were to capture who you are in a non-portrait painting, what would the painting look like?"

As clients try to answer these questions, the likelihood is that their answers are unrehearsed; they haven't had a chance to hear their answers in another setting and screen out threatening material; they are less certain where this material will lead and what it will reveal. In short, they are less well defended.

Simply asking one of these questions does not guarantee that something good will develop. The counselor must still sift the material through theoretical filter systems. The skills of following an idea or statement until clients find themselves dealing with their "guarded" truths are still needed. But the chances of getting to this guarded material are enhanced if we can invent ways to bypass clients' well-developed defenses. This line of questioning often will bypass those defenses and give the counselor and client quicker access to material that otherwise will be avoided or undiscovered for months, if not years.

80

Humor in therapy is a tricky issue.

At times helping clients to see the humor in a situation which they seem to be taking too seriously can be very helpful. Being able to laugh with the client can create a special bond between you—pain or sadness are not the only grounds upon which you can meet. But one must be *very* careful. Clients are wearing their nerves on the outside of their skin, and they are *very* sensitive. The real danger is of clients thinking that you are laughing at them instead of with them. They easily can be hurt—and not tell you about it—so you must be particularly astute in this matter. The counselor being misunderstood is always something to guard against. Humor is a very special area for this concern.

Still another aspect to watch for with humor is how the client uses humor as a part of his or life-style. Many very funny people use their humor to keep things safe, or at a distance, or to put people down, or to be likable, or to avoid further exploring of an issue, or all of these and more. With this kind of client, the counselor must be particularly careful not to be seduced by this kind of humor. A counselor can so easily enjoy such clients; they are such a relief from the anger or fear or sadness that usually live with clients. But the counselor's responsibility is to work with their clients and help them become aware of and stop whatever they are doing to avoid truth.

To allow humorous clients to use humor with us as they do with others is to contribute to the delinquency of clients. Call the process, find the truth, and go forward from there.

81

**To the largest extent possible,
make the counseling session an experience
of the client's life
rather than a story about it.**

Clients expect to tell you about their lives and generally are very good at doing it. With their life story they are usually the victim of others or of circumstances, and they are very well defended against their story being changed. A major contribution of Moreno with psycho-drama and Fritz Perls with Gestalt therapy was the introduction of dramatizing a situation, making it happen as though it were in the present with all emotions and behaviors of all people involved. Making it happen in the "here and now," making it real is something clients have usually not rehearsed before and are not as well defended against, as they are with their "story." In their dramatization clients will often become caught up emotionally in the event, and surprising data comes into the scene that otherwise might be forgotten or glossed over. Playing the role of another and playing it very well often helps clients become aware of how much the other person is really a creation of their own biases and expectation—their own myths. Simply and calmly talking *about* them doesn't have nearly the same effect. Hearing and seeing *how* they said something is often very different from what they said. Dramatizing their behavior often illustrates their life-style. Simply describing their behavior is nowhere near as vivid or informative. These are reasons for dramatizing the counseling interview. Dramatization is one way of capitalizing on the HERE AND NOW! It isn't the only way, however. We'll discuss more in this book.

82

Here and Now: The great mystery.

So much has been written about the Here and Now and so little is understood that I hesitate to add my words to the attempt to explain this all-important factor of counseling. But an understanding of the Here and Now and how to use it is an absolute necessity if one aspires to be a successful counselor. So I will try.

At this moment, in this room, I am perceiving, thinking, feeling, believing, behaving. Some of this I am aware of; much of this I am not aware of. What I am perceiving, thinking, feeling, and believing provide the bases of my behavior, of my existence. If I am to understand myself, at any given moment, I must be aware of what I *am* (right now, in this room) perceiving, thinking, feeling, believing and how this *is* effecting my choices for behaving. And if I can fully understand myself at any given moment, I can probably come to understand my entire lifetime. It is all one package.

Most people try to understand who they are right here, right now, by looking to their history. They look for causes and effects, for what used to be true and what the implications of this are for the present. They behave almost as if they are guessing about what is because of what was—even though "what is" is staring them in the face. Perhaps this is a safer way to try and understand. Perhaps people believe they can better handle "what is" about themselves if they put the distance of "there and then" into the picture. I personally believe that this is a part of it—not all of it, but an important part of it.

One of the things I try to do in counseling is put a strong emphasis on the here and now, on what *is* in the counseling session. My questions, my comments, my interest, all tend to direct clients to fully experience what they are in during the immediate moment. Gestalt therapy techniques are one way I do this. Focusing on how the client is interacting with me is another. Picking patterns of past behavior and finding them in the client's present relationships is still another. But no matter how I manage to do it, getting the client to be aware of his or her present perceiving, thinking, feeling and believing is my goal. In the present, these can be explored, challenged, accepted or changed—and only in the present! This is why the Here and Now is so important: it is the present script or life-style that is causing the client pain; this script is maintained by the present perceiving, thinking, feeling, believing; and only the present "stuff" can be changed.

I realize that the present is a continuation of the past; I realize that the past has its own importance. I make great use of the past in my counseling, as I describe in another part of this book. But if I have to choose between the There and Then and the Here and Now, Here and Now wins every time.

83

The famous "chairs," and how to introduce them.

I believe that when most people think of Gestalt Therapy, two things come to mind: (1) Fritz Perls and (2) his famous chairs. The use of two or more chairs to represent splits or polarities in the client, unfinished business between the client and some other significant person or persons, or even a device for the client to deal with strong feelings he or she might have toward the therapist. These are a stroke of genius. The chair technique is a kind of mini-psychodrama in which the client plays all the parts. The strength of this technique is that it creates an experience for the client instead of allowing him or her to narrate the "stuff" of therapy; and creating an experience instead of just talk intensifies feelings, breaks through defense mechanisms, and focuses the client on aspects of self of which he or she is unaware or is glossing over. The chair technique is probably the one Gestalt technique I use more than any other, and success with this technique is the rule rather than the exception. So I want my students to learn to use it.

However, most students counselors do not take the time to carefully introduce the chair technique to their clients. As a result clients balk at saying things to an empty chair; and the first few times student counselors try the chair technique they usually experience disaster. Introducing the chairs is crucial to their success, so I have developed an introduction that seems to elicit success instead of failure. It is as follows:

> **Counselor speaking to the client:** I imagine that you find yourself arguing both sides of this issue, in your head, over and over again, thus the issue remains unresolved. Is that right?
>
> **Client:** Yeah.

Counselor: Well, I'd like to hear the way you argue with yourself in your head, so that I understand your arguments better. But you will have to do the arguing out loud so I can hear it.

Client: Hmmm.

Counselor: In order to help me keep straight which side is arguing what, I'd like you to sit in this chair when you're on one side of the argument and then move to this other chair when you take the other side. That way I can see as well as hear where you are coming from at any one time. Does that make sense to you?

Client: Yeah. . .

Counselor: O.K. So why don't you start in this chair, and let me hear the way you keep yourself stuck.

What I am trying to do in this example is make talking to an empty chair seem to be a reasonable thing to do, and I am asking the client to do this as a means of *helping* me understand what the client is *already doing*, e.g., subvocalizing an argument in which the client is stretched in two directions. Presented in this way, clients rarely if ever refuse to cooperate in this exercise when it is first introduced. Their willingness to repeat the experience will depend upon how well the first experience is utilized. But that is another matter.

84

About-ism versus now-ism.

Something very different happens when a client tells about an incident or event versus having that event dramatized or actually take place during the interview itself. I call this about-ism versus now-ism. When clients are telling about an event they are usually calm and controlled. They often are simply relating information about an experience. When they are asked to dramatize an event, to make it happen in the office, to *be* the client in the circumstances *right now,* they do more than inform the counselor about pieces of history. The client is less passive and less controlled. Emotions are more powerful. Thoughts, fears, and intentions are more available. Unconscious motivation is brought closer to the surface. The intensity often catches the client by surprise and short-circuits defenses. A more total picture of the client and the event is brought into focus for both the client and the counselor to understand. The process is involved, not simply information. And the process is almost always the more meaningful.

The same now-ism exists when the counselor can capitalize upon the dynamics taking place between the client and counselor. These dynamics can often become the process to be intensified and then analyzed. The client's "being" is made the focus of the interview, which usually results in a far deeper understanding of the client than mere reporting of the "facts" about the client's life.

A variety of ways can be used to create and capitalize upon the now-ism which I've described. These ways include

1. working through the transference,

2. psycho-drama,

3. Gestalt techniques, and

4. dealing only with the present tense.

Whenever possible, I try to create a now-ism interview. It is almost always more productive than the about-ism interview.

85

You just had a thought. . . .

Over the years, as I worked with clients I became aware that clients' eyes moved a certain way when they had a new thought or a different train of thought. Sometimes they would then say something like, "I just remembered . . ." or "just had a memory . . ." or "I suddenly thought of . . ." But most of the time I would see the eyes move in a way that indicated a new thought or memory had occurred but the client would simply continue with what they had been saying. One day this happened and I interrupted the client with something like, "I believe that you just had a new thought, but that you didn't share it with me. What was that thought?" They did share the thought. It proved to be very important. So the next time I saw the eye movement I've described, I again interrupted and asked for the thought, the client shared it, and again it proved to be important. I have discovered that when the client has a new thought in the middle of what they are saying, most of the time the new thought is more important than what they are saying. And their eyes are the clue to their having this new idea.

What seems to occur is that in the course of the counseling dialogue, the resistance to an important repressed thought or memory is wakened enough that it comes floating into consciousness. It may or may not fit neatly into the ongoing discourse. If it fits, the client includes it in part of the dialogue, and the new idea becomes part of the work. But if it doesn't fit neatly into what is being said, the client will not share the thought. The client doesn't want to seem disjointed or incoherent. So the thought passes and may be lost from consciousness again. My experience is that it usually does not fit neatly into what is being said. Usually a connection can be made but it is seldom an obvious connection. And it is almost always worth pursuing.

Perhaps I have discovered a new way to accomplish what free association hopes to accomplish, i.e., short-circuit the repression of threatening material. Whatever it is, I find it very helpful. So whenever I see the eye movements which indicate a new thought has just "popped," I am apt to say, "You just had a new thought. Will you share it with me? "

86

And/But

Almost every sentence spoken during the counseling interview can be followed by either of the words "and" or "but." Many times the client does not want to expand the discourse about a certain subject, but I have a hunch that they should do so. By simply repeating the word "and" after they have completed their sentence and dropped their voice, they are easily directed to say more on the subject. Doing this four or five times is not at all unusual. Eventually the client learns to stop trying to minimize an important area.

I also have found that many times the client will discuss an area in one direction and I *know* they use it in another direction. By simply adding the word "but" when they want to stop the sentence they are easily led to go in the directions they are trying to avoid.

Certainly I'm not suggesting that the counselor use either the word "and" or "but" after every client statement; but knowing you can, if you want to certainly is nice; so you *know* you can do so almost any time you want.

87

Find out what is, not what isn't.

Clients have a variety of ways of talking that seem to communicate but in fact may be misleading or confusing. One of these ways is to tell the counselor what isn't rather that what is.

"I don't mind if she goes with him" is much different and safer than saying how he does feel about the situation.

"I don't care whether she likes it or not" is not as clear a message as saying, "I hope she gets angry about what I am doing."

"I'm not losing any sleep over this, you know," doesn't tell me much. I might say, "What are you doing instead?" Or "What *are* you losing sleep over?" can go much farther. . . .

"It doesn't matter to me what he does" is not as clear as how he does feel about what he does.

"I don't dislike her at all" still avoids committing himself to acknowledging how he *does* feel about her.

In each of these examples the client is trying to avoid revealing self or committing self to a position or a value, etc. The counselor can only go farther in the exploration of something that is true and it's up to the counselor to get the client to speak in a way that can be further explored or intensified.

88

When a client is talking about "people," they may be talking about you—check it out.

When I hear a client making statements about MEN, and "I'm a man," I ask, "Are you talking about me?" If the clients says, "No," then I ask, "Why not?" Oftentimes they are indeed including me, and that allows us to begin working on the "stuff" going on between the client and me, in the here and now. These dynamics are almost always very productive ones for the therapeutic process and I capitalize on them whenever possible.

Everything mentioned above can also apply whenever a client begins talking about "PEOPLE"; I'm a people, so I ask, "Does that mean me?" The client may well not realize that they are using a "safe" method to comment on or criticize the counselor. The client's responsibility is to spot the possibility and to use it in a responsible manner.

89

**Listen for a refrain.
It may give you a clue to their style.**

I believe that a person's manner of speaking is an indication of how he or she thinks, and how a person is thinking is important to me as a counselor. So I try to be very aware of people's speech patterns.

Some people make extensive use of the passive voice, which allows them to avoid allocating personal responsibility for what happens.

> "The radio was turned up loud" is much different than saying "I turned the radio on loud."
>
> "My car went through the red light" is not the same as saying "I drove through the red light." The client knows the difference, but at some level is trying to avoid responsibility.

Other speech patterns often prove to be important. Illustrations of some of these patterns are as follows:

> "I don't know" frequently asserted by the client is a means of not talking responsibility. How can you expect anything from someone who never knows anything?
>
> "I have to" usually means "I choose to, but I don't want to be blamed for my choices."
>
> Repeated use of "I can't" usually means the client is trying to avoid being held responsible for not wanting to.

> "She said. . ." "and so I/He did. . ." "and so I/They. . ." "and so I" are constructions which often indicate clients seeing themselves as only responding to what others do or say. Apparently they don't initiate anything.

> "What are you going to do?" implies that no reasonable person would expect them to try and change things.

These refrains and others like them are never accidental. Clients like to say that a speech refrain is only habit. I agree with them—but then I maintain that habits become habits because they accomplish something very well. Let's see what this habit is accomplishing.

90

When you make an intervention, pay particular attention to how the client defends against it—and then make another one!

One of the amusing things that happens very, very often with student counselors and their clients is that counselors will make interventions that they expect to be really significant and then they sit back and expect something wonderful to happen. What does in fact happen is that clients ignore, deflect, or disarm interventions and counselors are flabbergasted. Student counselors simply do not appreciate how skilled their clients are at being themselves and how experienced they are at fending off attempts to change things.

I attempt to teach my students that an intervention rarely does enough by itself. The cumulative effect of many interventions is what is going to help clients make changes in their lives that need to be made. Many small steps were taken so that clients could become what they are. Many more small steps will be needed to bring about change. Further, I want counselors to make interventions and then watch like hawks as to how clients defend against them. Then counselors should either make a mental note about that defense so that they can deal with it later, or side-step around the defense with a second intervention. When counselors make interventions they must be especially alert to the situation. They cannot sit back complacently and expect something wonderful to unfold.

91

To make the client's material meaningful, intensify, intensify, intensify.

The difference that a client experiences when talking to a counselor instead of a friend or neighbor is not so much due to what the client says but what the counselor *does* with what the client says. The friend or neighbor is apt to listen to what the client is saying; the counselor is more apt to get the *client* to listen to what the client is saying: to listen, to experience, and to get greater meaning than ever before..

I do this in a variety of ways:

1. When clients speak about a class or group of people, I will often ask them to pick one person, use that person's name and deal with this individual in a specific way rather than generalizing.

2. When clients say statements that seem to be particularly important, I often ask them to repeat a statement several times, more emphatically each time, with greater intensity in their voice or in their gestures. We then see if this has made a difference.

3. I will often exaggerate, to the nth degree a client's words or conclusions, e.g., I made statements such as "this is my destiny," "there is no escape, there are no options," "all I can do is live this way and suffer," and "I am truly a blameless victim. . ."

4. When clients are complaining about a particular aspect of their life I sometimes ask them to brag about this aspect and tell the world how clever they are to make things be this particular way. Then we see if this bragging fits better than the complaint.

5. If clients are sitting in an unusual posture or using unusual gestures or choice of words, I often ask them to stop and look at me as I mirror them; we then see if they can give meaning to what I am mirroring.

6. A question that often is very productive goes something like this, "Right here, right now, at this moment as you are talking to me, what are you experiencing?"

7. When clients wants to tell me about an event that they believe is very significant to them, I often ask then to dramatize the event in a mini psychodrama, or to use the famous Gestalt chairs and "be" the people in the event as though it was happening at this moment.

What all of the preceding suggestions have in common is the facility to intensify what clients are saying so that they can hear themselves in new and different ways and to see some meanings between the lines that were too faint to discern in normal discourse. More often than not, new insight will be forthcoming.

92

Confrontation does not mean aggression!

Most students who come into counselor training are caring, nurturing people who like human relationships and enjoy living with others in a harmonious manner. Confrontation is not something student counselors value highly. They do not enjoy nor are they highly skilled at "winning the battle"; that is probably one reason they are students of counseling rather than student attorneys. So I find that most of my students avoid confronting their clients as practicum begins. Getting them to be appropriately confrontive is often a difficult thing to teach, largely because of how they unconsciously define "confrontation." When I ask them to consciously define the term, they usually speak about starting an argument or getting their client angry or being aggressive about a point they are insisting upon—or similar kinds of thinking. When I redefine the term and give the students wide latitude in ways of putting the definition into action, appropriate confrontation begins to happen.

I define confrontation as

1. asking your client to make sense out of what seems to be contradictory material they have told you—not as a challenge but as your attempt to understand,

2. getting your clients to look at things in their lives that they have successfully been avoiding—not by force but by persuasion,

3. asking your clients to clarify issues that are confusing to you but that apparently are not confusing to them, and

4. telling your clients something that you believe is true and asking them to respond—not as something to argue about but as an attempt to share different perceptions of what we believe is true.

None of the preceding necessitates being aggressive; none of the preceding implies being hostile or angry. Nor do they imply eliciting aggression, hostility, or anger from your client. On the contrary, to be successful, confrontation must be experienced by clients as the counselor's attempt to understand them or attempt to help them understand themselves, and *this can't happen if the client is angry or hostile.* So don't avoid confrontation! Find ways to be confrontive that fit your personality and still do the job when it is necessary.

93

Subvocalization—you can't stop it, but you must change it.

Albert Ellis, in his Rational Emotive Therapy, stresses the part that subvocalization plays in continually re-indoctrinating the individual to his or her belief system. This is *such* an important concept, and I think it is neither well understood nor capitalized upon by many counselors. While I am not an advocate of Albert Ellis or his style of counseling, I do believe he is absolutely right about the importance of subvocalization and I try to teach this importance and what to do with it.

People are always talking to themselves subvocally. We all do it. Our thoughts are subvocalized, continuously, and the subvocalized messages trigger new thoughts which become subvocalized which trigger new thoughts ad infinitum. We seem to develop shorthand kinds of subvocalizations in response to repeated situations such as meeting new people. The subvocalization may be, "They are probably thinking how tall I am and how skinny I look." Each of us has our own repertoire which we carry around with us and play to ourselves as familiar circumstances arise. Very often these subvocalizations are quite helpful, as we instruct ourselves in how to behave under certain circumstances. The trouble starts in counseling when these subvocalizations pop into the client's mind in situations that have been troublesome in the past and to which we are trying to develop new and better kinds of responses. The old self-instructions tend to trigger the old responses and neutralize the new learnings. I teach my clients to deliberately talk to themselves (as they used to do as children) in these new ways of thinking and behaving and to argue with their old subvocalizations when certain situations arise. We must short-circuit these old automatic instructions that clients give themselves, or they will keep themselves stuck in their old ways. This is a very tedious part of the counseling process. It is also a very frustrating part because the old self-instructions are so automatic and so well learned. But these old myths must be replaced with new ones. Knowing with what they must contend is crucial for the beginning counselor.

94

Another perspective. . .

As is evident in the many other topics in this book, I put a great emphasis on the unconscious component of counseling and on this transference phenomenon and how to use it. Certainly a conscious component also is present—a relationship between the client and the counselor that is in fact between the client and the counselor. This conscious, present relationship also can be a tool for the counseling process. It can provide another *perspective* from which to view the undistorted past and present, another perspective for giving meaning to reality, another perspective in putting together the bits and pieces of one's life.

Assuming the counseling process has developed well, at some stage in the relationship the client will view the counselor as a unique kind of trusted confidant. In this stage, which I believe comes in the latter part of counseling, the counselor can comment on his or her own view of the client's data—not to convince, but to consider. The client has been so locked in to a particular way of defining and conceptualizing own world that another view of that world may be helpful. This must be handled with great care and concern. The client is very vulnerable and has given the counselor an enormous amount of trust. So I deliberately use such phrases as "just another way to think. . ." or "another way to view that. . ." or "from another perspective. . . ." I want to give the client the opportunity to experience a dialogue where both people can think out loud about something, without the need to win or lose or to defend their position. From this kind of dialogue grows client confidence in self and perhaps a new and better way of relating to others.

95

Suicide: I always take it seriously.

In twenty years of private practice I have never had a client commit suicide. I have had only two clients put under 24-hour supervision to preclude the possibility of suicide. So obviously, suicide or attempted suicide is *not* an everyday occurrence. But a consideration of suicide by a client is *not* a rare thing, either; and whenever the client mentions suicide, no matter how vaguely, I consider it a very serious matter. Successful suicide is one of the few things in life you can't change your mind about later. As a counselor I may get only one chance to deal with the idea in an individual client, and I never allow the opportunity to slip by me by accident.

If the client mentions suicide, I stop all other discourse and deal with this issue. I tell my clients that of course they have the power to take their lives. To pretend otherwise is foolish. But since they can always make that decision any time they wish, let's save that option until we have tried many other options first. We both can laugh a little at that, and then I become very serious. I *do* believe that suicide is a viable option for all of us. At times suicide might make sense. But because it is indeed the last choice one can make, I really want to save it for the last and look at other options very carefully. If, after exploring all other options, suicide still seems the best choice, then the client may indeed kill self.

Once a client makes up his or her mind to kill oneself, unless under close supervision the chance of preventing the suicide is very small. My best chance of helping such a client is to get to the person before the decision is made. addressing the issue the very first time a client alludes to it has been successful for me. Perhaps I've just been lucky. If so, I'm glad.

SECTION VII

DO and DON'T

96

Ask broad questions about narrow subjects.

One of the "tricks of the trade" that I have developed has to do with the kind of questions I ask my clients. I ask broad questions about very specific subjects.

> Instead of asking, "How many brothers/sisters do you have?"
>
> > I say something like, "Tell me about you and your brothers/sisters."
>
> Instead of, "Was your relationship with your mother a happy one?"
>
> > I ask, "What can you tell me about you and your mom?"
>
> Instead of, "Were you a good student in high school?"
>
> > I ask, "When you think of high school, what comes to mind?"
>
> Instead of, "Do you like people?"
>
> > I ask, "How would you describe you and other people?"

The advantage of my kind of question is that it gives the client a very specific area on which to focus (which I am good at picking) but allows them great freedom to move toward the aspects of the topic that are significant (which I am less able to pinpoint). Because of my filter system (which I discuss in another section of the book), I have little difficulty moving to areas to explore; but I leave the client the freedom to sort out the significant stuff within each area—which only the client can know.

When you ask a question you run the risk of taking your client away from the right track to the wrong track, because your question determines the track you take. I'm quite confident in picking the right area to question, so I am willing to limit my client to a very specific topic. I am far less confident about what "stuff" within that topic is important to deal with, so I make that part of my question as broad as possible. I pick the track. he picks the direction, the speed, and the destination.

97

A great answer to a different question.

Many clients have absolutely amazing skill in avoiding the painful areas of their life that must be acknowledged before therapeutic gain can be achieved. Nowhere is this more evident than the skill they display in avoiding direct questions about a part of their life they prefer you don't ask. Rarely do they tell you not to ask that question. Instead they give you a very interesting answer that has nothing to do with your question. And if their answer is interesting enough, you may not realize that your question has been avoided. Politicians do this with reporters all the time and we smile when we see it happening, but I don't smile when I see a student counselor so easily handled. If you have asked a good question, be sure you get an answer to that question.

98

K-I-S-S. *Keep It Super Simple.*

A scene that I watch develop each semester of practicum is one in which a student counselor explains something to a client, and the client seems confused, so the counselor explains it again; only this time the counselor speaks a bit louder, a bit slower, and uses longer sentences. Keep it simple! Use sentences instead of paragraphs, and keep the sentences as short as possible whenever you have to explain or teach something to your client. If you find yourself involved in making long, involved explanations, you're doing something wrong. Either the client is playing stupid so that you have to work harder, or you're not firmly grounded in what you are trying to say. If you find that you make similar explanations or statements to many of your clients, develop your sketch outside the interview, practice it, and keep it short and sweet. In any case, if the client seems confused, get less wordy, not more wordy. Let the client do more of the work in understanding.

99

Spontaneity may mean you are unprepared!
Rehearse some scenes at home.
Develop mini-lecturettes for certain subjects.

Some scenes repeat themselves from client to client; some subjects seem to appear in many counseling relationships. I urge my students to recognize these and practice or rehearse their half of these scenarios in private or at home. Why create their part of the scenario in the heat of the action? Get it down pat and be able to spend energy observing the client.

I think the counselor should have several ways of beginning the counseling relationship; three or four will be enough for most counselors. These openings should be smooth and professionally presented. The client will respond better to a well developed opening than to a counselor who seems unsure of self and who appears awkward at the beginning of the relationship.

Topics such as blame, guilt, and embarrassment come up over and over again. The counselor certainly can be prepared as to how to comment when any of these topics arise. Sexuality and self-esteem are always a part of the counseling dialogue. The counselor should have know several phrases that will open these sensitive subjects with as little tension as possible. Introducing some exercises such as those found in Gestalt therapy can be rehearsed ahead of time by the counselor. I think having prepared lecturettes about personal mythologies and present choices, ready to insert into the counseling session is perfectly realistic. If they have been rehearsed, they are more apt to be succinct and clearly stated rather than ambiguous and diffused. Prepared lecturettes also are apt to be shorter in length than are the wandering explanations which are created on the spot.

The typical reaction I get when I first suggest that student counselors should rehearse certain scripts at home is disbelief. The second reaction is usually more negative than that. Somehow, if something is rehearsed, that means it is phony. Sincerity seems to be synonymous with spontaneity. *Nonsense.* Sincerity has *nothing* to do with spontaneity. Sincerity has only to do with heart-felt truth. The fact that a person has cared enough to find exactly the right way to say something that he or she knows will be said is an indication of willingness to work at doing something right. In many cases spontaneity is more an indication of being unprepared or of an unwillingness to do one's homework than it is of being sincere. In the heat of battle is no time to develop the subtle nuances that are so important to success of the counseling process. In the quiet of one's home may be just such a time.

I am not suggesting that one is able to "can" the counseling interview. I am not suggesting that the counselor throw in "comment 14" when the client emits a particular cue. But I am suggesting that with situations that repeat themselves across many counseling relationships, the counselor may do a better job if prepared to respond in a way that has been well thought out and well developed, than if the counselor tries to wing it and goofs—particularly if the same situation is goofed with several clients.

100

Body language—the least well defended.

I would guess that Fritz Perls did more to make mental health professionals and the world at large aware of body language than any other individual. I can remember, very vividly, the first time I saw Fritz working with one of my students. Fritz focused a great deal on the client's hands. The hands did exemplify what Jim was experiencing—far more accurately than Jim's words. It was a real lesson for me in the importance of resistance and the need to lower and/or end-run the resistance factor. Working with the body language is one way to do this.

I believe that body language is an effective means of getting around the resistance factor because it is largely out of conscious control and conscious rehearsal by the client. The client is unaware of the body language and what it means and where it will lead, so he or she is less able to defend against it. Things "pop" through—or bubble through—but material comes to the fore because it is so unexpected.

Most verbal material is carefully monitored by the client before it comes out of the mouth. Most of what comes out of the mouth has come out before, and the client knows what the implications are and where the line of talk is apt to go. The client is forewarned, so to speak, and definitely is on guard. Depending only on the client's well guarded verbal behavior really puts the counselor at a disadvantage and prolongs the counseling process. I have come to believe that many successful therapists and counselors have developed ways of talking with clients that differ from how most of us talk with friends. The now famous client-centered "reflection" is certainly not normal conversation; the analytic "free association" is certainly not normal conversation. Because these methods are not normal ways of conversing, I believe that the client's defense mechanisms—which are geared for normal discourse—are less effective, and repressed material sneaks through. So, too, with capitalizing on body language. The client is less well defended with the unrehearsed, unnormal material which flows from the focus on body language. Less defended material is apt to be more significant material as the counseling process uncovers the forgotten myths by which the client lives his or her life. Do focus more on body language.

101

Talking "about" feelings without having feelings is seldom helpful.

One of the more common events that take place between client and counselor is talking about feelings in a very non-feeling way. Doing so is seldom helpful to anyone. I believe this is true because it is normally a time when the client is talking about history (recent or long past); historical feelings being described are really no different than describing historical events or people—informational but not process. As I have said elsewhere, information in counseling becomes significant only when the counselor can use it to create meaningful experiences for the client, through which the counseling process can occur. The client must feel something *right now* if it is going to mean anything. So I may ask clients to put that feeling in their voice or their gestures; I may ask them to put an event in the present tense and make it real for themselves *in this moment;* I may ask them to put an event or situation into a kind of psychodrama and feel the appropriate emotions *in context.* But whatever I do I will try to get the client to stop talking about feelings and to feel them.

102

Counseling is not a social dialogue—don't be polite.

Time after time I have sat and watched student counselors sit and allow clients to talk and talk ad infinitum. When asked why they didn't interrupt and do something with what had already been said, they inevitably answer that they didn't want to be rude. Or when I ask why a student counselor didn't ask specific questions about such things as a client's sexual behavior, they are apt to answer that they didn't want to appear nosey.

Let me make this absolutely clear. As a counselor your job is to interrupt your client, at times. Your responsibility is to ask personal questions of a sensitive nature. Social convention does not apply to the counseling interview. You are not to be limited by what is appropriate for the friend or neighbor. Clients seem to understand this better than many student counselors.

10

Don't ask "why," ask "what."

One of the most common mistakes the student counselor makes is to ask the question, "Why?" This question can mean either (1) what was your intention or (2) what was the cause for your behavior. Most of the time the client will interpret this to be asking about the cause of his behavior, and this usually elicits justification and rationalization on the client's part—something of which the counselor has too much already. Asking about intentionality is usually far more productive. All important behavior is intentional and has an objective in mind. This is where you will find the "good stuff" for your client. So don't give your client the opportunity to rationalize or justify behavior with "because. . . ." This is the client's strong suit. The client has these "reasons" down pat already. Ask about intentions; hold the client accountable for those intentions; and you will move closer to those hidden truths about which I'm always talking.

104

One question at a time.

A common mistake that student counselors make is to ask too many questions at one time. Clients are not helped by asking several questions together such as the following:

> "What do you think that means? I mean, do you think it was an accident? Are you satisfied with what happened?"

All of the above questions are asked before the client has answered any one of them. Each of them may be a good question, but we will never know; they are all asked like a machine gun. If the counselor asks a question and the client doesn't answer immediately, the counselor frequently asks another question (thinking, perhaps, that the first question wasn't understood). Don't do that! If you ask a question, wait for the answer. If the client doesn't answer, find out why. But don't assume that the question was misunderstood. Clients may hesitate to answer a question because they must think about how to answer, or they may be hoping they don't have to answer, or any number of things. If clients discovers that when they pause before answering a question, the counselor will ask another question, they clients have learned a way to avoid the counselor's intervention.

Another problem with asking several questions in rapid sequence is that the client really may not be sure which question to answer first. Or, worse yet, each succeeding question interrupts the client's thoughts of the preceding question, which defeats the purpose of asking any question.

So make sure that you know what you want to ask, word the question carefully, and wait for an answer. It sounds simple, but the mistake of sequential questions is so common that it obviously is not simple. Remember that you are teaching the client to be your client. Don't teach them to wait until they get the question *they* want.

105

If you ask a question, don't you answer it.

Another common mistake I see student counselors making is that of answering their own questions. When I ask students to explain this behavior, I hear such explanations as the following:

> "I don't know. . ."
>
> "I thought maybe I had asked the question poorly."
>
> "The client looked confused, so I helped him/her out."
>
> "I was afraid I had embarrassed the client, so I demonstrated that the answer was nothing new to me by answering it for him/her."
>
> "I was showing the client how well I understood him/her. .(?)"
>
> "I was tired of his/her evasive answers."
>
> "I was hoping that was the right answer so I could lead to something."

None of the above justifies supplying the answer to your own questions. A lawyer often does this with justification. But never a professional counselor! Ask your questions because you need to know something you don't know. Don't use a question in order to make a statement. Don't take your client off the hook, if the question is a good one. Don't try to save a bad question by answering it yourself. Simply ask your question and wait for a reply. If one is not forthcoming, find out why.

106

The client may be trying to entertain you—or himself/herself.

Don't be fooled into thinking that the client will automatically be talking about that which is really significant. Some student counselors are afraid to interrupt the client or get them off their train of thought. There are some times when that is a legitimate concern. But more often than not, clients will be talking about things they enjoy talking about, or things they are practiced at talking about, or things they imagine the counselor will find enticing. Listen to the voice, watch the body language, and listen to the rhythms of speech. Shortly after a client begins to talk about something, you should begin to see and hear signs that this will supply significant data. If you don't, the chance is good that it is not significant. I often ask clients how this topic is significant to their lives. If it isn't, I ask them to pick a topic that is. Much to the surprise of my students, clients usually do.

107

Watch for the tears behind the laughter.

Laughter can be a very therapeutic tool, if used carefully by the counselor. But laughter must be watched very carefully. The client so often laughs when nothing is funny; and inappropriate laughter is always an indication of substituting laughter for some other reaction—usually either anger or tears. Don't allow your clients to laugh, or even smile, at inappropriate times. They are using the laughter or the smile to conceal something—not only from you but from themselves. Whatever they feel is necessary to cover up is probably important to look at and experience.

If laughing or smiling in a given circumstance seems to me to be inappropriate, I ask clients to help me understand the laughter or the smile. If they can show me the humor in the situation (and they seldom can), I drop the subject and we carry on. Otherwise, I ask them to repeat what they were saying and leave out the smile or the laughter. A more valid, appropriate emotional response will usually come to the surface. Sometimes I have clients repeat what they were saying several times, first with and then without the laughter, then with and then without. The client will usually experience the difference, and we take it from there.

Don't allow your client to cover up the truth. You're in the truth business. Allowing them to laugh inappropriately contributes to the delinquency of your client.

108

If you miss an important dynamic or piece of information, don't worry! If it is important,it will come up again.

Most student counselors live in fear that they will miss *THE* important detail of the client's narrative that will make the difference between the success or failure of the counseling. As a matter of fact, they *generally do* miss many important details that can make a difference in the success of their counseling. Fortunately, they always get several chances at any truly important detail—as long as the client keeps coming.

Anything that is indeed significant about the client will be involved with the client and the client's life-style. People, events, or circumstances become important only as they relate to the clients being themselves. As the counselor works with the client being oneself, sooner or later the important aspects of being the client will come into view—those people, events, or circumstances will continue to reappear in one form or another until they are dealt with. I guarantee it! So while I am not advocating sloppy attention to detail by the counselor, I am advocating less apprehension about missing and losing the one opportunity for success. Not just *one* opportunity exists. What is important will continue to reappear in one form or another until we find it—as long as the client keeps coming to counseling.

SECTION VIII
TERMINATION

109

**How do you end an interview?
One way is to say STOP!**

Next to starting an interview, the most common problem for beginning counselors is stopping it. Once clients start talking about themselves and realize the counselor is really listening to them in a nonjudgmental, accepting way—it is pretty heady stuff. The client likes it, and often isn't ready to stop when the session should be over. But they *must* stop. The session is allotted so much time and no more. Other clients are waiting to see the same counselor or to use the same office. You have to get the client out of the office.

But the client isn't the only problem. The student counselor is often the one who keeps the session going beyond the allotted time. Once the client is talking, the counselor often is afraid to stop—maybe the client won't start again. Or the client is really interested in what is developing and the counselor can't find a "natural" stopping place. So the counselor waits until "it" happens. Or the counselor really has the client moving and is intensely interested in what happens next. Or the client finally reaches an intensive situation during the last ten minutes of the session, and the counselor can't stop now.

Yes, you can! And you must! Not only is stopping on time important because other people are waiting for their turn; once you start letting the clients run over the allotted time, they will unconsciously start saving "the good stuff" until the end of the session—whenever that may be. Studies done in the 1960s found that clients tend to pace themselves and use the last 20 minutes of the session to really work. If the session was 40 minutes long, they used the last 20 minutes. If the session was 60 minutes long, they used the last 20 minutes. If the session was 90 minutes long, they used the last 20 minutes. So train your client to know that the session is so many minutes long and then stick to that time frame.

Equally important is the issue of controlling the counseling session. Some clients are having trouble in their life because they attempt to control all of their relationships. This kind of client will inevitably try to control the counseling relationship. One way of doing this is to control the length of time the interview lasts. Of course other ways exist but for now I'm emphasizing controlling the ending of the session. In general, termination of the counseling session must remain the responsibility of the counselor.

So how do I end the session? I say such profound things as the following:

> "I think we should stop now."
>
> "This seems like a good place to stop for today."
>
> "I can see that we are in the midst of painful material, but our time is up. You're probably going to think about this a great deal between now and next week."
>
> "I see we have about ten minutes remaining before we stop." (Ten minutes later I use one of the above statements.)
>
> "Our time is up. . .I can see that you're not done yet, but we must stop for now."

Some clients, particularly those who want to control things, *won't* stop when I say any of the preceding. They are incredible. They ignore the terminating words and they ignore the nonverbal cues on my face and in my eyes that accompany termination. With this kind of client I say, firmly: "I'm going to stop now"—and *I stand up* and if necessary walk toward the door. I've never had a client ignore these cues. Talk about needing a club! But sometimes the strong message must be sent. The counselor must be willing to send it.

Of course, at times the counselor will find that running over the time allotted is necessary. Occasionally, to stop the interview simply because the clock says so is impossible or even unwise. These situations do occur, *but not very often.* In my own practice, I don't go beyond the allotted time more than once or twice a year. It simply isn't necessary more often than that. Student counselors who run over time twice in two weeks are doing something wrong.

110

When are you ready to stop counseling?

Such a question would seem to be an easy one, but the answer is a bit complex. Such a thing as "flight to health" can confuse the issue. At times, when things start getting very painful or quite sticky, clients may suggest that you have been a big help, they have wonderful new perspectives on things, and they won't be needing counseling any longer. This flight to health is *not* rare, and the counselor should not give approval to this attempt to avoid what is coming next in the counseling process. Obviously, if clients are determined to terminate, they have the right and the power to do so. But very often they won't terminate at this point, if the counselor does not agree with their assessment of the situation. So the counselor must be careful that he or she does not contribute to the delinquency of the client by agreeing to a termination that is really a flight from the truth.

On the other hand, the time does come to terminate. Usually clients and counselors recognize this time together. The client isn't living a perfect life, but a sense of strength and competence to face the truth is more than the client had previously. A new kind of equality exists between client and counselor that is hard to define but is nevertheless very real to both counselor and client. Things are ready for termination when the client can truthfully paraphrase with something like, "Life is not perfect, but basically I am OK, people are OK, and I can live my life honestly and openly and expect to be OK most of time."

One final word about termination. I am afraid that some counselors would like to make a career out of a few clients; and some clients might be willing to allow this to happen. Stopping too soon must be guarded against. So too, must we guard against failing to terminate when it is warranted. So you see, the answer to the question is indeed a bit complex.

ABOUT THE AUTHOR

JIM CARNEVALE

Jim Carnevale was born and reared near Buffalo, NY. After a four year enlistment in the navy, he moved to Southern California where he received his B.A. in English from U.C.L.A. (1957) then he received an M.S. in Counseling from San Diego State University (1961) and later attended University of Southern California where he received his Ph.D. in Counseling (1968). Dr. Carnevale has been a teacher for more than 30 years: 6 yrs high school English; 4 year Jr. College English; 21 years as a professor of Counseling at San Diego State. During his tenure at San Diego State, Dr. Carnevale was also a therapist in private practice; and it was his experiences as a therapist that led him to specialize in teaching practicum—"where students really learn to become counselors."

Dr. Carnevale and his wife live aboard a 40′ sailboat and are avid sailors and skiers. They hope to retire soon and sail their boat to Europe for "as long as it is fun."